PEARSON　　　　　ALWAYS LEARNING

Phlebotomy Technician Program
Student Workbook

Third Custom Edition for
Condensed Curriculum International

Excerpts taken from:
PowerPoint Slides to accompany Phlebotomy Handbook:
Blood Specimen Collection from Basic to Advanced, Ninth Edition
by Diana Garza and Kathleen Becan-McBride

ISBN 10: 1-323-40915-7
ISBN 13: 978-1-323-40915-2

TABLE OF CONTENTS

PART A
Phlebotomy Technician

STUDENT PACKET INFORMATION

TABLE OF CONTENTS

The Phlebotomy Technician Program

COURSE DESCRIPTION

Phlebotomy is an integral part of the diagnosis process. It has been said that 80% of diagnosis of disease is achieved through laboratory analysis. As a phlebotomist, you will play an important role in the healthcare field. Obtaining an accurate specimen to ensure quality results is vital to your success. This course will teach you the skills necessary to performing this valuable function.

The Phlebotomy Technician Program prepares professionals to collect blood specimens from clients for the purpose of laboratory analysis. Students will become familiar with all aspects related to blood collection and develop comprehensive skills to perform venipunctures completely and safely. Classroom work includes terminology, anatomy and physiology; blood collection procedures; specimen hands-on practice; and training in skills and techniques to perform puncture methods. The program also includes lab exercises, blood draws, work with a training arm and other exercises intended to prepare students to function as an entry level Phlebotomy Technician.

EXPECTATIONS FOR THE STUDENT

1. Students are expected to arrive for class on time

2. Absent students must contact their instructor prior to class time

3. Absent students will be expected to make up missed class work/assignments on their own time

4. Students will follow the rules and regulations of the facility

5. No student shall disrupt a class or interfere with the session or the learning or the other students

6. The Instructor will be the student's contact for all academic questions or concerns

7. Cell phones and pagers are to be turned off or to the vibrator mode while in class

8. Any student participating in any act of academic dishonesty, such as cheating, plagiarism, or collusion will be considered for dismissal from the program. Once dismissed, no condition of re-entrance will be considered.

TEACHING METHODS EMPLOYED

Lecture, class discussion, group discussions, role-playing, critical thinking exercises, and application activities.

EVALUATION AND GRADE DETERMINATION

Student performance will be evaluated utilizing the following analysis:

- Attendance and class participation (50%)
- Quizzes (25%)
- Final Exam (25%)

It is vital that each student recognize that this class is <u>a pass/fail class</u>.

SYLLABUS

The attached syllabus provides a class-by-class outline of the materials to be discussed during class as well as the homework assigned for the following class. This syllabus is a guideline and may be adjusted to the needs of the class at the discretion of the instructor.

PHLEBOTOMY TECHNICIAN
SYLLABUS

Instructor: _____

Contact: Phone _____

                                    E-Mail _____

Class Time: _____

Required textbook:

1. **Phlebotomy Handbook**, Ninth Edition; Author: Diana Garza and Kathleen Becan-McBride

2. **Phlebotomy Technician Program Student Workbook**

The course outline attached will indicate the information that will be covered in each class and what homework assignment will be required for the next class. This syllabus is subject to revision based on the needs of the class.

The students are responsible for the following:

- All homework assignments and preparation is to be completed prior to class.
- Students are responsible for all homework assignments, scheduled quizzes and tests, and hands-on experience (if applicable). If any of these is missed due to absenteeism or tardiness, the student is responsible to make up the missed work to successfully complete this course.
- Contact your instructor if you have any anticipated student absenteeism.
- Student effort and commitment is necessary to understanding the course materials. It is strongly recommended that all course materials be reviewed and studied prior to and following each class.

PART B
Phlebotomy Technician

STUDENT HANDOUTS –
PHLEBOTOMY REVIEW

TABLE OF CONTENTS

The Phlebotomy Technician Program

Student Handout #1

PHLEBOTOMY PRACTICE AND QUALITY ASSESSMENT

The phlebotomist's role is ever changing. Below is a list of the duties and responsibilities associated with the phlebotomist's role today:

- Prepares the patient for collection procedures associated with laboratory samples
- Collects routine skin punctures and venous specimens for testing as required
- Prepares specimens for transport to ensure stability of sample
- Maintains patient confidentiality
- Transports specimens to the laboratory
- Comply with all procedures instituted in the procedure manual
- Promote good public relations with patients and hospital personnel
- Assist with collecting and documenting monthly workload and recording data
- Maintain safe working conditions
- Perform laboratory computer operations
- Participate in continuing education programs
- Collect and perform point-of-care testing (POCT)
- Perform quality control checks on POCT instruments
- Perform skin tests
- Process specimens and perform basic laboratory tests
- Collect urine drug screens
- Perform electrocardiography (if required by position)
- Perform front office duties, current procedural terminology coding and so on

GENERAL PRACTICES OF PHLEBOTOMY

Definition: The term is derived from the Greek language, phleb which relates to veins, and tomy which relates to cutting. Venesection/venisection are synonyms of phlebotomy.

Function

- Primary function of the phlebotomist is to provide accurate, safe, and reliable collection and transportation of specimens to the clinical laboratory

Purpose

- Diagnostic Testing
- Therapeutic assessments
- Monitoring of patient's health status

PUBLIC RELATIONS AND CLIENT INTERACTION

As a member of the clinical laboratory team, the phlebotomist plays an important role in public relations for the laboratory. A confident phlebotomist with a professional manner and a neat appearance helps to put the patient at ease and establish a positive relationship. The following lists attributes that are necessary to achieving this goal.

Professional Behavior

- Sincere interest in health care
- Accountability for doing things right
- Dedication to high standards of performance
- Propensity for cleanliness
- Pride, satisfaction and self-fulfillment in the job

Effective Team Member

- Understand the mission
- Know basic skills for group processes and team dynamics
- Understand relevance and commitment to team goals
- Be reliable and dependable
- Communicate ideas and feelings
- Participate in decision making
- Be flexible in decision making
- Constructively manage conflicts
- Contributes to the cohesion of the team
- Contributes to problem-solving strategies
- Supports and encourages other team members

The following are the medical facilities where the phlebotomist may find work:

- Physician office laboratories – can range from simple screening tests done in a single practice office or specialized testing done in large group practices.

- Reference laboratories – these large independent laboratories perform routine and highly specialized tests that cannot be done in smaller ones. The phlebotomist may do either on-site or off-site collections.
- Urgent care centers
- Nursing home facilities
- Wellness clinics

HEALTHCARE DELIVERY

Two general categories of facilities, inpatient (non-ambulatory) and outpatient (ambulatory), support all three levels of healthcare presently offered in the U.S. They are:

1. Primary Care – offer routine care such as the primary care physician who assumes ongoing responsibility for maintaining patients' health

2. Secondary Care – a physician or specialist who performs routine surgery, emergency treatments, therapeutic radiology, and so on

3. Tertiary Care – highly complex services and therapy level practitioners that usually require the patient to stay overnight such as acute care hospitals, nursing homes and extended care facilities

DEPARTMENTS WITHIN THE HEALTHCARE FACILITY

Hospitals are often large organizations with complex internal structures. The following lists the most common departments found.

Health Care Departments

- Geriatrics – Elderly
- Oncology – Cancer
- Proctology – Lower Bowel
- Rheumatology – Arthritis
- Family Medicine
- Neonatal – Infant
- Physical Medicine
- Plastic surgery

Medical Departments

- Orthopedics
- Ophthalmology
- Otolaryngology
- Urology
- Cardiology
- Dermatology
- Neurology
- Hematology

Ancillary Departments

- Laboratory
- Occupational therapy
- Physical therapy
- Nuclear medicine
- Electroencephalography (EEG)
- Pharmacy
- Nutrition
- Radiology
- Electrocardiography (ECG or EKG)
- Radiotherapy

Other Support Services

- Housekeeping, maintenance
- Security, purchasing
- Laundry, information services

Ambulatory Care

- Hospital based clinics
- Physician group practices
- Rehabilitation centers
- Free standing surgical centers
- Mobile vans for blood donations

Long Term Care Facilities

- Nursing home
- Assisted living
- Retirement Communities

CLINICAL LABORATORY

The clinical laboratory is divided into two major divisions:

1. Anatomical and Surgical Pathology
2. The Clinical Analysis Areas

ANATOMICAL AND SURGICAL PATHOLOGY

This section of the laboratory performs the following functions: tissue analysis, cytogenic examinations, surgery biopsies, frozen sections, and performance of autopsies. The laboratory departments associated with this section are:

- Histology – defined as the study of microscopic structures of tissues
- Cytology – studies the cells in body tissues and fluids
- Cytogenics – studies specimens for chromosomal deficiencies

CLINICAL PATHOLOGY

This section of the laboratory performs the following functions:

- Specimen processing, hematology analysis, chemistry analysis, microbiology analysis, blood bank/immunohematology analysis, immunology/serology analysis, and urinalysis testing.

COMMON LABORATORY TESTING

The following describes each of the departments located within the clinical pathology area and the tests that are most commonly performed in that department.

Clinical Chemistry – The most automated section in the laboratory. This section is divided into several areas:

- **Electrophoresis** – analyzes chemical components of blood such as hemoglobin and serum, urine and cerebrospinal fluid, based on the differences in electrical charge.

- **Toxicology** – analyzes plasma and urine levels of drugs and poisons.
- **Immunochemistry** – this section uses techniques such as radio immunoassay (RIA) and enzyme immunoassay to detect and measure substances such as hormones, enzymes, and drugs.
- Some tests in the chemistry section are ordered by profiles, which are groups of tests ordered by a physician to evaluate the status of an organ, body system or general health of the patient. Examples of these profiles are:
  - Liver profile: tests may include ALP, AST, ALT, GGT and Bilirubin
  - Coronary risk profile: tests may include Cholesterol, Triglycerides, HDL, LDL

Hematology/Coagulation

This is the section where the formed elements of the blood are studied by enumerating and classifying the red blood cells, white blood cells, and platelets. By studying and examining the cells, disorders and infections are detected and treatment instituted or monitored. Whole blood is the most common specimen analyzed and usually collected in lavender-top tube containing the anti-coagulant EDTA.

Aside from complete blood count (CBC), which is the primary analysis performed, other tests such as: Erythrocyte sedimentation rate (ESR), Lupus erythematosus (LE) prep, Reticulocyte (retic) count, and Sickle cell. The coagulation section is usually a part of hematology. However, in large laboratories they are separated. This is the area where hemostasis is evaluated. Plasma is usually the specimen analyzed drawn from blood collected in light-blue top tube with the anticoagulant sodium citrate. The tube must be inverted three to four times. Some of the tests frequently performed in the coagulation area are: Activated partial thromboplastin time (APTT); Thrombin Time (TT); Prothrombin time (PT); Bleeding Time (BT).

Blood Bank Section

This is the section where blood is collected, stored and prepared for transfusion. Strict adherence to procedures for patient identification and specimen handling is a must to ensure patient safety. Blood collected may be separated into components: packed cells, platelets, fresh frozen plasma, and cryoprecipitate.

Serology (Immunology) Section

Performs tests to evaluate the patient's immune response through the production of antibodies. This section uses serum to analyze presence of antibodies to bacteria, viruses, fungi, parasites and antibodies against the body's own substances (autoimmunity).

MICROBIOLOGY SECTION

This section is responsible for the detection of pathogenic microorganisms in patient samples and for the hospital infection control. The primary test performed is culture and sensitivity (C&S). It is used to detect and identify microorganisms and to determine the most effective antibiotic therapy. Results are usually available within 24 to 48 hours; but cultures for tuberculosis and fungi require several weeks. One instance when culture and sensitivity is used is to diagnose the cause of a patient's fever of unknown origin (FUO).

URINALYSIS SECTION

This section performs tests on the urine to detect disorders and infection of the kidney and urinary tract and to detect metabolic disorders such as diabetes mellitus. Urinalysis has three components:

- Physical examination – evaluates the color, clarity and specific gravity
- Chemical examination – determines pH, glucose, ketones, protein, blood, bilirubin, urobilinogen, nitrites, and leukocytes.
- Microscopic examination – identifies presence of casts, bacteria, yeast, and parasites

LABORATORY PERSONNEL

The clinical laboratory team is comprised of many different personal, they are as follows:

- Pathologists
- Administrative staff
- Technical supervisors
- Laboratory information system analysts
- Clerical staff
- QA staff

- Medical Technologists (MT)
- Medical Laboratory Technicians (MLT)
- Infection control staff
- Clinical Laboratory Scientist (CLS)
- Phlebotomists

NATIONAL STANDARD AND REGULATORY AGENCIES

The main key players in bringing quality improvement to healthcare are:

1. **Joint Commission on Accreditation of Healthcare Organization (JCAHO)** – establishes standards for hospital operation and is an accrediting agency for healthcare facilities

2. **College of American Pathologists (CAP)** – the CAP and Accreditation Program is an accreditation for laboratory services

3. **Clinical Laboratory Improvement Amendments of 1988 (CLIA)** – federal regulatory system to establish national standards for laboratory testing

4. **Clinical and Laboratory Standards Institute (CLSI)** – recognized as the authority for laboratory guidelines and operating procedures

QUALITY ASSURANCE

Quality assurance (QA) is defined as a program that guarantees quality patient care by tracking the outcomes through scheduled audits in areas of the hospital that look at the appropriateness, applicability, and timeliness of patient care. A QA program is a continuous program, established by the healthcare facility, which will provide guidelines, protocols and continuing education for their employees. Areas in phlebotomy that are subject to quality control.

Quality Management Is Most Commonly Identified with 3 Components

- STRUCTURE: facility, staff and management structure
- PROCESS: process assessment to gauge the appropriateness of what was done for the pt
- OUTCOMES: cure rates, pt. Satisfaction, nosocomial infection rate, and recovery rates

Quality Monitoring

- TQM (Total Quality Management) – ongoing and involves all levels of healthcare
- CQI (Continuous Quality Improvement) – continuous program to improve quality
- QC (Quality Control) – monitors a process, developing policy and procedure
- QI (Quality Indicators) – processes that have been identified as key components are continuously monitored for level of quality

QCI FOR PHLEBOTOMY

Areas in phlebotomy that are subject to QC are:

- Response time
- Patient wait time
- Time required to complete venipuncture
- % of successful venipunctures on first try
- # of venipuncture attempts on average per pt
- # and size of hematomas and TAT

QC FOR PHLEBOTOMY

Quality control checks and preventative maintenance to include:

- thermometers
- BP cuffs
- centrifuges
- Testing of the centrifuge for RPMs using a tachometer. Specimens are usually centrifuged at 850 to 1000g
- When testing BP cuffs for slow leaks, the mercury should not change by more than 5 mm Hg/sec

QI FOR PHLEBOTOMY

Competency and performance assessment include:

- universal precautions
- knowledge of policy and procedure
- pt. ID procedure
- customer service skills
- team building skills

CLIA (CLINICAL LABORATORY IMPROVEMENTS)

CLIA was developed and adopted in 1988 and became law in 1992. Its purpose is to regulate and provide standards for all laboratories to regulate the quality and accuracy of laboratory testing. It is administered by the Centers for Medicare and Medicaid (CMS). The following describes its functions:

- establishing qualifications for lab staff
- periodic inspections
- proficiency assessments
- investigations of complaints

Patient Preparation Procedures

Quality control actually starts before the specimen is collected from the patient. To obtain an acceptable specimen, the patient must be prepared properly. In a hospital setting the phlebotomist must check the floor book, to ensure that the nursing department has performed all pre-test preparations. Pre-test preparation will include fasting for specific tests. The phlebotomist must then ensure this information is correct, by asking the patient. The Laboratory/Phlebotomy Specimen Collection Procedures Manual has established these guidelines.

COMMON PHLEBOTOMY QUALITY CONTROL INDICATORS

Before Collection	During Collection	After Collection
Patient misidentification	Extended tourniquet time	Failure to separate serum from cell
Improper Time of Collection	Hemolysis	Improper use of serum separator
Wrong Tube	Wrong order of draw	Processing delays
Inadequate fast	Failure to invert tubes	Exposure to light
Exercise	Faulty technique	Improper storage conditions
Patient posture	Under filling tubes	Rimming clots
Poor coordination with other treatments		
Improper site preparation		
Medication interference		

Quality Frameworks

- **Six Sigma** – a method designed to improve process performance by reducing variation, improving quality, enhancing financial performance, and improving customer satisfaction. It provides a data driven, systematic approach to quality management through five phases:
  - Define
  - Measure
  - Analyze
  - Improve
  - Control
- Clinical Laboratory Standards Institute (CLSI) has established 12 quality system essentials (QSEs)
    Policies – indicate intentions, for example "what we do"
    Processes – activities required to implement qualities policies
    Procedure Documents – instructions for performing steps
  - Documents and records
  - Organization
  - Personnel
  - Equipment
  - Purchasing and inventory
  - Process control
  - Information management
  - Occurrence management
  - Assessments (external and internal)
  - Process improvement
  - Customer service and satisfaction
  - Facilities and safety

The Phlebotomy Technician Program

Student Handout #2

COMMUNICATION, COMPUTERIZATION, AND DOCUMENTATION

COMMUNICATION SKILLS

Phlebotomy is both a technical and a people-orientated profession. Many different types of people or customers interact with phlebotomists. Favorable impressions result when professionals respond properly to patient needs. The following describes the communication process:

The three components of communication are:

- Verbal communication
- Nonverbal communication or body language
- Active listening

Common communication terms are:

- Kinesics – use of body language in communication
- Proxemics – non-verbal communication involving a person's use and concept of space
- Kinesic Slip – when verbal and non-verbal communication does not match
- Filter – barriers in communication
- Tone – pitch of voice

VERBAL COMMUNICATION

Effective communication involves:

- Show empathy
- Show respect
- Build trust

- Establish rapport
- Listen actively
- Provide feedback

Barriers to Effective Verbal Language

- Using medical terminology
- Hearing Impairment
- Language other than English
- Age
- Tone of Voice

- Emergency Situation
- Different generations – Veterans (up to mid 40's), Boomers (40's – 64), Generation X (65–81), Generation Y (82–2000)

NONVERBAL COMMUNICATION

Positive body language involves:

- Maintaining erect posture
- relaxed hands and smiling face
- Communicating face to face at eye level

- Maintaining eye contact and zone of comfort (18" to 4')
- Displaying good grooming habits

Negative body language involves:

- Rolling of eyes or looking away
- Sighing deeply
- Chewing gum

- Tapping foot, fingers or pencil
- Thumbing through books or papers

COMPUTERS IN HEALTHCARE

Today, healthcare is very dependent on the computer. Laboratory information systems are the backbone for ordering analysis as well as documenting testing results.

In the laboratory setting, it is common for laboratories to use the Bar Code system for labeling specimens. This system creates a label similar to the barcode we find on the items we purchase each day. The computer recognizes these codes and assigns an accession number to each test ordered. The computer then generates a label for this test indicating all the necessary information required by the phlebotomist to obtain the specimen. Once the specimen is obtained the phlebotomist transports it to the lab where the bar code is scanned and the computer receives the message that the specimen is in the lab and ready for analysis. Once the analysis is completed the computer interfaces with the instruments and enters the results for that barcode into the computer where it is accessed by the ordering physician.

WHAT IS A COMPUTER?

A computer is a device that accepts information and manipulates it for some result. Computers can be confusing, and it takes a little time before you gain confidence in using and understanding them. Just like a new TV or VCR, computers can be a bit cumbersome to figure out, but once you achieve a certain level of knowledge, these machines can become powerful allies.

The illustration below lists the most common component of a computer

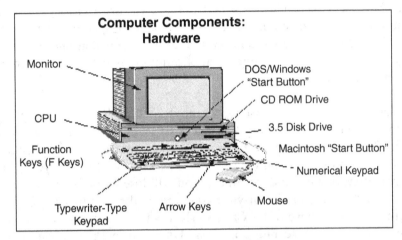

3 1/2″ disk drive—drive that allows you to use 3.5 disks

Arrow keys—used to help locate certain spots on the window or desktop

CD ROM drive—drive that allows you to use CD's

CPU—Central Processing Unit—case or housing for internal operating mechanisms

Function (F) Keys—shortcut keys (depending on software)

Keypad—similar to a typewriter keyboard

Monitor—for viewing computer operations

Mouse—used to help locate and activate certain things on the computer

Numerical keypad—a calculator-type area for numerical entering

Start buttons—buttons used to turn the computer on

COMPUTER BASICS: WHAT DOES THAT COMPUTER TERM MEAN?

Just about every profession has its own special terminology, and computer users are no different. In fact, they generate more confusing jargon than most other fields. Unfortunately, specialized terminology can confuse the non-specialists. Here are several of the most common computer terms that you are likely to come across.

- **Application/program** – a specially designed piece of <u>software</u> created to do a specific task or function, like word-processing, spreadsheets, creating graphics, etc., Examples would be programs like Word, Word Perfect, and Excel.
- **CD-ROM** – is an abbreviation for Compact Disc, read-only-memory. It is another storage device for files, such as a <u>Floppy disk</u>. Currently most CD's will not use this term, but instead will be called CD-R (for readable only), or CD-RW (for readable/writable). Readable only means that you can only save information to it once and that unlike a floppy it can't be reused over and over again. Readable/writable means that you can save information and then delete it and reuse the disk. You must use a software application to "burn" or write/save information to a CD and you must have a CD drive that is also a CD-RW drive sometimes called a "CD Burner". Unlike Floppies, CD's can come in various sizes indicated by the number of MEGs (i.e. 700 megs, 800 megs, etc).

- **CPU** – Central Processing Unit. This is the brain of the computer. Information will usually be printed, displayed on the screen, or saved either to the hard drive or a disk (<u>Floppy</u> or <u>CD</u>).
- **Crash** – a computer crash or the expression "my computer has crashed" usually means either your screen has frozen or you have reached a blue screen/error message. If a program has frozen, but your mouse/pointer can still move try to go to another open program and close it. Often a computer will freeze if there are too many applications opened at once and it runs out of memory (<u>RAM</u>). *Note: Closing some unused applications may help free up resources and your program may unfreeze.

Another thing you can do if your mouse won't move is close the "crashed" program. In most new Windows system clicking the following key once, Ctrl+Alt+Del will bring up a Windows Close Program dialogue box. Simply highlight the program you want to close and click the End Task button. A second message may pop up saying the program is not responding, do you want to end program, click yes. Unfortunately, this method may mean you will lose all of your unsaved work. Also, make sure you don't hit Ctrl+Alt+Del twice or your computer will reboot/restart. If you have crashed and reach a blue screen you may have to hit Ctrl+Alt+Del twice in order to reboot your machine. It will then restart and go through a scanning process. Let it finish this scan as it may prevent future problems.

If this happens to you on a regular basis, using different programs, you may have to invest in additional memory.

- **Cursor** – is a visual indicator (usually represented as a blinking line in text programs or as an arrow) on the screen that lets you know where your <u>mouse</u> is positioned. On a web page the cursor usually turns into a pointing hand when positioned over a button or link that when clicked on will take you somewhere new. The cursor allows you to insert text where you wish, or to select existing items to be deleted, copied, or modified in some way.
- **Desktop** – in a <u>Windows</u> environment, the desktop is the view on the monitor that you usually see after starting the computer and after the Windows screen has loaded. It displays your <u>icons</u> and shortcuts. Most desktops will have at least an icon for My Computer (links to all of the drive letters of your computer), a Recycle Bin (garbage can where files are stored when you delete them until you choose to "Empty your Recycle Bin" at which point they are actually gone) and My Briefcase (a place to store files for later retrieval or movement).
- **Drive** – any part of the computer where disks reside and operate, temporarily or permanently. See <u>floppy drive</u>, <u>CD drive</u>, and <u>hard disk/hard drive</u>. You may also have a tape drive for backing up materials such as a ZIP drive.
- **File/Document** – any single item created with an <u>application</u>, this can be anything that is saved to your computer, such as a paper, a spreadsheet, pictures, sounds, and downloaded programs (although usually documents only refer to items with text).
- **File Server or Server** – a large capacity computer which is connected to other computers for the purpose of sharing information and processing ability. For example, a university department might use a file server for documents or projects that are worked on by multiple users on different computers in the same building. Another example would be a web server. This is a server that holds web documents that are accessible through the Internet to other computers. File servers are often part of a <u>network</u>.
- **Floppy Disk/Diskette** – is a flat, portable, disk made of plastic that can store files written magnetically on its surface. Information stored on Floppy disk can be read, copied, or deleted. The disk is protected by a shell or cover of some kind. "Floppy" is now a misnomer, it was originally referred to an obsolete type of disk 5.25" disks were actually flexible or floppy, while new ones, 3.5" disks, are not. To open or read a Floppy a computer or laptop must have a Floppy Drive. Many new computers and laptops do not include Floppy drives since they are now considered obsolete now that most new systems include <u>CD burners</u>. Laptops may have swappable drives,

where a user must remove and replace a modular CD drive with a floppy drive. *Note: some speakers and paperclip holders have magnets, don't store floppy disks next to them or they can be damaged or erased/demagnetized.

- **Gig** – refers to the amount of memory or space, when used to describe data storage. One Gig or gigabyte is equal to 1,024 megabytes. Gigabyte is often abbreviated as G or GB. (1 MB is equal to 1,048,576 bytes. Megabyte is frequently abbreviated as M or MB.)
- **Graphic User Interface** – also called a GUI, this is a system where things are shown graphically. This means that instead of entering commands on a text only screen with a keyboard, the user manipulates icons and windows, often with a mouse.
- **Hard Disk/Hard Drive** – this is a permanent storage unit containing a disk or disks that are made from metal. Most computers have built-in hard drives. Hard drives contain the long term memory of your computer. Some users may also have external hard drives for storage of large numbers of files or as a method of back-up. This is a hard drive that plugs into the computer, usually through a USB connection.
- **Hardware** – the physical components of a computer, including cables, the keyboard, the CPU, monitor, etc.
- **Icons** – pictures that are shortcuts to programs or files. By clicking on an icon, you start the program or open the file.
- **Initialize/Format** – these terms are synonymous, occasionally it may also be referred to as reformatting if you are doing it for a second time, such as reformatting a floppy to reuse it or reformatting a computer to delete all information from the hard drive. After formatting a disk, whether it is a floppy or hard disk, it is necessary to put some files back on before the disk can be used again. You never want to format a computer unless you know what you are doing. You may want to format floppy disks in order to reuse them.
- **Meg** – refers to the amount of memory or space, when used to describe data storage. 1 MB is equal to 1,048,576 bytes. Megabyte is frequently abbreviated as M or MB. (One Gig or gigabyte is equal to 1,024 megabytes. Gigabyte is often abbreviated as G or GB.)
- **Modem** – is a device that plugs into a standard telephone jack and allows a computer to transmit and receive information over commercial telephone lines. There are also different kinds of modems that use other delivery systems instead of a phone line, like cable modems. Another type of device is a NIC or Network Interface Card, which is used for networks like LANs and WANs.
- **Monitor** – the screen on which you see your work, whether in color, grayscale, or black-and-white. Color monitors can show from 16 to over a million different colors. The other important setting in monitors is the resolution. The resolution of a monitor indicates how densely packed the pixels (colored dots that make up an image) are. In general, the more pixels, the sharper the image will be. Most modern monitors can display 1024 by 768 pixels. Some high-end models can display 1280 by 1024, or even 1600 by 1200. Color and resolution can be changed on a computer. Changing factory settings may seriously impact how small icons and other things look on your desktop. Make sure you know what you are doing before you change these settings.
- **Mouse** – a small tool that duplicates the movements of your hand on the computer's screen, allowing you to rearrange items, perform actions, select things, etc.
- **MP3** – this stands for "MPEG-1 Audio Layer-3" and is a digital, compressed music file (these files always end with an .mp3). MP3 files are often downloaded or exchanged between people online. To hear these files you must use a player. Most newer Windows operating systems come with an MP3 player pre-installed, otherwise there are free players available online for download. There was some controversy in the music industry over downloading copyrighted music and companies such as Napster who once provided free downloads, now often require a fee to download music, unless otherwise expressed.
- **Network** – a group of computers spread out over a large area that are connected with each other, whether by telephone lines, fiber-optic cables or some other linkage. Once connected, computers on a network can share files, send large amounts of information very quickly, and

enable multiple users to communicate at the same time. These are usually further defined as a LAN or a WAN. **LAN** stands for a Local Area Network (LAN) and WAN for a Wide Area Network (WAN). WANs are usually created for large geographical areas and typically consist of two or more LANs.

- **NIC** – an abbreviation for Network Interface Card, this is a card inserted into your computer or laptop that allows it to communicate with a network, usually a LAN or a WAN. A type of NIC that is specifically made for LAN's is called an Ethernet card and it comes in several different connection speeds. A NIC is connected to a special network outlet with a cord that looks like a little bit like a fat phone cord. (This cord is called a CAT5 or category 5 cable).

- **Operating System or Platform** – these terms refer to the software that your computer uses to operate (otherwise known as your OS) and not to a manufacturer or company. Windows 2000, Windows XP, and OSX (Mac) are common platforms.

- **Peripherals** – are devices connected to a computer which aren't a part of the main machine. Examples are a mouse, speakers, keyboards, printers, scanners, etc.

- **RAM** – Random Access Memory, the computer's "short term" memory used whenever an action is performed by a program. It is also called the "active memory". RAM is what the computer uses to run all applications. The amount of RAM in your computer is fixed, but it can be increased. It is one of the two kinds of memory that dealers will use to describe a computer's capabilities. Programs will often specify that a certain amount of RAM is required in order for the application to run correctly. RAM is usually specified in <u>Megs or MB</u>. (The other kind of memory dealers refer to is "storage" memory or hard drive size. It usually is specified in <u>Gigs or GB</u>.)

- **ROM** – Read-Only Memory, in which information is saved once and can never be altered. For example, CD-ROM drives read information saved on compact disks (CD's). A CD-ROM drive can read that information, but cannot make changes to it, for that you need a CD-RW drive. Some ROM is built into your computer to help it get started when you turn it on.

- **Software** – also called an application, this is any information a computer uses to perform a task; also, any information saved on a disk.

- **System** – specific pieces of software that your computer needs to run. For example, it is the system which converts your typed keystrokes into letters displayed on a monitor screen.

- **Teleconferencing** – is to hold a conference using a telephone or network connection. Computers have given new meaning to the term because they allow groups to do much more than just talk. Now a teleconference can include sharing an application, files, and a bulletin board like space where a user can display slides, comments, or files. There are many teleconferencing applications that work over private networks, one of the earliest was Microsoft's NetMeeting. See also <u>video-conferencing</u>.

- **USB** – stands for Universal Serial Bus (the plug is very flat and has no pins or prongs). This is a style of port connection that is used by many <u>peripheral</u> devices such as Palm Pilots, phones, scanners, printers etc. This type of connection is much faster than more traditional kind of connections such as serial and parallel ports (often used by older printers these ports have plugs with little screws attached).

- **Videoconferencing** – is related to teleconferencing, but more involved. Usually it means two or more participants at different sites are connected by using computer networks to transmit audio and video data. For example, a point-to-point (two-person) video conferencing system. Each participant has a webcam/video camera, microphone, and speakers connected to his or her computer. As the two participants speak to one another, their voices are carried over the network and delivered to the other's speakers, and whatever images appear in front of the video camera appear in a window on the other participant's monitor.

- **Webcast** – "Webcasting" is a term that describes the ability to use the Web to deliver live or delayed versions of sound or video broadcasts.

- **Windows** – this term can be confusing. The same term refers to several different things. One is a graphic way of displaying information on a screen, in windows, that allow you to view the contents of each window as if they are loose pages on a desk that can be shuffled around. Windows are very useful because they can be opened, closed, stacked, sorted, resized, and moved, so you can move very quickly from one application or file to another.

A second thing that Windows refers to is a series of operating systems sold by the Microsoft Corporation called "Windows ___" (i.e. Windows ME, Windows XP, etc.). These are operating systems that show information in a graphic interface format, complete with <u>icons</u>, mouse cursor, etc. Finally, applications are sold that call themselves windows-based. This means they work within a windows environment or operating system. A Mac user must use mac-based programs.

DOCUMENTATION

A requisition form must accompany each sample submitted to the laboratory. This requisition form must contain the proper information in order to process the specimen. The essential elements of the requisition form are:

- Patient's surname, first name, and middle initial.
- Patient's ID number.
- Patient's date of birth and sex.
- Requesting physician's complete name.
- Source of specimen. This information must be given when requesting microbiology, cytology, fluid analysis, or other testing where analysis and reporting is site specific.
- Date and time of collection.
- Initials of phlebotomist.
- Indicating the test(s) requested.

An example of a simple requisition form with the essential elements is shown below:

```
┌─────────────────────────────────────────────────────────┐
│ LABORATORY SERVICE – UNIVERSITY OF UTAH HOSPITAL        │
│ Patient Name: _____ │
│ Patient ID: _____ │
│ Patient Birthdate: _____ Sex: _____      │
│ Source of Specimen: _____ │
│ Date Collected: _____ Time: _____ Phleb: _____ │
│ Physician: _____ Location: _____       │
│ Diagnosis: _____ │
│ Tests Requested:                                        │
│                                                         │
│ _____ Electrolyte Panel      _____ Complete Blood Count │
│                                                         │
│ _____ Hepatic Panel          _____ Protime / PTT        │
└─────────────────────────────────────────────────────────┘
```

Patients' Medical Record

- Can be a clinical (written) record or electronic medical record (EMR)
- Legal document that provides a chronological log of care
- Protected by confidentiality law called Health Information Portability and Accountability Act (HIPAA)

The Phlebotomy Technician Program

Handout #3

PROFESSIONAL ETHICS, LEGAL, AND REGULATORY ISSUES

ETHICS AND PHLEBOTOMY

Ethical behavior entails conforming to a standard of right and wrong to avoid harming the patient in any way. Standards of right and wrong called the "code of ethics" provide personal and professional rules of performance and moral behavior that all phlebotomists are expected to follow. The process of phlebotomy can present an ethical situation for any phlebotomist. When faced with this situation, ask the following questions:

- Is this legal or does it comply with policy?
- Does it foster a win-win situation?
- How would I feel if I read about this situation in the paper? How would my family feel?
- Can I live with myself after making this decision?
- Is it right?

Bioethics is one of the largest ethical issues debated today due to the use of human stem cells for biotechnology research.

Basic Legal Principles

- Criminal Law – concerned with laws that are designed to protect all members of society from injurious acts by others

- Civil Law – is concerned with actions between two private parties
- Tort – a civil wrong committed against a person or property that results in proven damages
- Assault – the act (threat) of intentionally causing another to be apprehensive of immediate harm to his or her person
- Battery – intentional harmful or offensive touching of another person without consent or legal justification
- Fraud – willful plan to produce unlawful gain
- Invasion of Privacy – a violation of one's right to be left alone
- Breach of confidentiality – failure to keep medical information confidential
- Discovery – examination of witnesses prior to a trial

PATIENT CONFIDENTIALITY

Patient confidentiality is defined as:

- No one except the patient may release patient results without clinical need-to-know

MALPRACTICE

Defined as: improper or unskillful care of a patient by a member of the health care team, or any professional misconduct or unreasonable lack of skill.

STANDARD OF CARE

Defined as: all healthcare workers perform their duties in the same fashion that any reasonable person with the same experience and qualification in the national community.

RESPONDEAT SUPERIOR

Defined as: an employer must conform to specific standards of care to protect patients and must answer for damages committed by an employee.

VICARIOUS LIABILITY

Defined as: persons hired as independent contractors are personally liable for their actions.

STATUTE OF LIMITATION

Defined as: establishes a particular number of years within which one person can sue another.

PATIENT CONSENT

There are several different types of consent:

- Informed – voluntary and competent written permission for a medical procedure
- Expressed – may be given verbally or in writing

- Implied – the patient need not make verbal consent, the patient's actions implies consent i.e. a patient holding out their arm for a blood draw
- HIV consent – patient is given counseling and signed consent is obtained
- Consent of minors – anyone under 18 must have consent from parent or guardian
- Refusal of Consent – patient has a right to refuse treatment

Legal Cases Involving Phlebotomy Procedures

- Jones vs. Rapides General Hospital – pt was stuck with the same needle twice
- Congelton vs. Baton Rouge General Hospital – patient received injury of antebrachial cutaneous nerve from donation of blood
- Montgomery vs. Opelousas General Hospital – patient received damage from a blood draw
- Martin vs. Wentworth Douglas Hospital – patient received damage to nerve during blood draw

INFORMED CONSENT

This is consent given by the patient who is made aware of any procedure to be performed, its risks, expected outcomes, and alternatives.

NATIONAL RESEARCH ACT

Regulates the collect of blood from patients and other individuals for research purposes.

PATIENT CONFIDENTIALITY

This is the key concept of HIPAA. All patients have a right to privacy and all information should remain privileged. Discuss patient information only with the patient's physician or office personnel that need certain information to do their job. Obtain a signed consent form to release medical information to the insurance company or other individual.

NEGLIGENCE

This is the failure to exercise the standard of care that a reasonable person would give under similar circumstances and someone suffers injury because of another's failure to live up to a required duty of care.
The four elements of negligence, (4 Ds), are:

1. Duty: duty of care.

2. Derelict: breach of duty of care.

3. Direct cause: legally recognizable injury occurs as a result of the breach of duty of care.

4. Damage: wrongful activity must have caused the injury or harm that occurred.

TORT

Is a wrongful act that results in injury to one person by another. Some examples of common torts that can occur in the clinic are the following:

Battery – the basis of tort in this case is the unprivileged touching of one person by another. When a procedure is to be performed on a patient, the patient must give consent in full knowledge of the procedure and the risk it entails (informed consent).

Invasion of privacy – this is the release of medical records without the patient's knowledge and permission.

Defamation of character – this consists of injury to another person's reputation, name, or character through spoken (slander) or written (libel) words.

Good Samaritan Law – this law deals with the rendering of first aid by health care professionals at the scene of an accident or sudden injury. It encourages health care professionals to provide medical care within the scope of their training without fear of being sued for negligence.

PATIENTS BILL OF RIGHTS – DEVELOPED BY THE AHA THROUGH "THE PATIENT CARE PARTNERSHIP"

As a Patient in XXX Hospital You Have the Right, Consistent with Law, To:

1. Receive treatment without discrimination as to race, color, religion, gender, national origin, disability, or source of payment.

2. Receive considerate and respectful care in a clean and safe environment free of unnecessary restraints.

3. Receive emergency care if you need it.

4. Be informed of the name and position of the doctor who will be in charge of your care in the hospital.

5. Know the names, positions and functions of any hospital staff involved in your care.

6. Receive complete information about your diagnosis, treatment and prognosis.

7. Receive all the information that you need to give informed consent for any proposed procedure or treatment. This information shall include the possible risks and benefits of the procedure or treatment.

8. Receive all the information you need to give informed consent for an order not to resuscitate. You also have the right to designate an individual to give this consent for you if you are too ill to do so.

9. Refuse treatment, examination, or observation, if retired or a family member, and be told what effect this may have on your health.

10. Refuse to take part in research. In deciding whether or not to participate, you have the right to a full explanation.

11. Privacy while in the hospital and confidentiality of all information and records regarding your care.

12. Participate in all decisions about your treatment and discharge from the hospital.

13. Review your medical record without charge. Obtain a copy of your medical record for which the hospital can charge a reasonable fee. You cannot be denied a copy solely because you cannot afford to pay.

14. Receive a bill and explanation of all charges.

15. Complain without fears of reprisals about the care and services you are receiving and to have the hospital respond to you; and if requested, a written response. If you are not satisfied with the hospital's response, you can complain to the Patient Representative Office located here in the hospital.

16. Receive information about pain and pain relief measures, be involved in pain management plan, and receive a quick response to reports of pain.

17. Receive healthcare in an environment that is dedicated to avoiding patient harm and improving patient safety.

18. The right to request information about advance directives regarding your decisions about medical care.

19. Make known your wishes in regard to anatomical gifts. Your may document your wishes in your health care proxy or on a donor card, available from the hospital.

20. Understand and use these rights. If for any reason you do not understand or you need help, the hospital will attempt to provide assistance, including an interpreter.

PATIENT RESPONSIBILITIES

- **Provision of Information:** You have the responsibility to provide, to the best of your knowledge, accurate and complete information about present complaints, past illness, hospitalizations, medications, and other matters relating to your health. You have the responsibility to report unexpected changes in your condition to the responsible practitioner. You are responsible for making it known whether you clearly comprehend a contemplated course of action and what is expected of you.

- **Compliance with Instructions:** You are responsible for following the treatment plan recommended by the practitioner primarily responsible for your care. This may include following the instructions of nurses and allied health personnel as they carry out the coordinated plan of care and implement the responsible practitioner's orders, and as they enforce the applicable hospital rules and regulations. You are responsible for keeping appointments and, when you are unable to do so for any reason, for notifying the responsible practitioner or the hospital.

- **Refusal of Treatment:** You are responsible for your actions if you refuse treatment or do not follow the practitioner's instructions.

- **Hospital Rules and Regulations:** You are responsible for following hospital rules and regulation affecting patient care and conduct.

- **Respect and Consideration:** You are responsible for being considerate of the rights of other patients and hospital personnel and for assisting in the control of noise, smoking and the number of visitors. You are responsible for being respectful of the property of other persons and the hospital.

PATIENT REPRESENTATIVE

The Patient Representative's primary assignment is to assist you in exercising your rights as a patient. He/she is also available to act as your advocate and to provide a specific channel through which you can seek solutions to problems, concerns and unmet needs.

THE PATIENT BILL OF RIGHTS FOR PAIN MANAGEMENT

You have the right to:

- Information about pain and pain relief
- A caring staff who believe your reports of pain
- A care staff with concern about your pain
- A quick response when you report your pain

You have the responsibility to:

- Ask for pain relief when your pain first starts
- Help those caring for you to assess your pain
- Tell those caring for you if your pain is not relieved
- Tell those caring for you about any worries that you have about taking pain medications
- Decide if you want your family and/or significant others to aid in your relief of pain

The Phlebotomy Technician Program

Student Handout #4

INFECTION CONTROL

INFECTION CONTROL/CHAIN OF INFECTION

This consists of links, each of which is necessary for the infectious disease to spread. Infection control is based on the fact that the transmission of infectious diseases will be prevented or stopped when any level in the chain is broken or interrupted. Candida albicans is the most commonly identified pathogenic microorganism that causes health care-associated skin infections. Herpes virus is another commonly identified pathogen that affects skin.

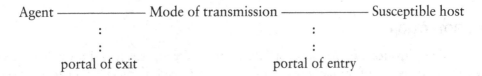

Agent ——————— Mode of transmission ——————— Susceptible host

portal of exit   portal of entry

Agents – are infectious microorganisms that can be classified into groups namely: viruses, bacteria, fungi, and parasites. When infectious diseases are identified according to the specific disease-causing microorganism, the disease may be prevented with the use of anti-infective drugs or infection control practices.

Portal of Exit – the method by which an infectious agent leaves its reservoir. Standard Precautions and Transmission-Based Precautions are control measures aimed at preventing the spread of the disease as infectious agents exit the reservoir.

Mode of Transmission – specific ways in which microorganisms travel from the reservoir to the susceptible host. There are five main types of mode of transmission:

- Contact: direct and indirect
- Droplet
- Airborne
- Common vehicle
- Vectorborne

Portal of Entry – allows the infectious agent access to the susceptible host. Common entry sites are broken skin, mucous membranes, and body systems exposed to the external environment such as the respiratory, gastrointestinal, and reproductive. Methods such as sterile wound care, transmission-based precautions, and aseptic technique limit the transmission of the infectious agents.

Susceptible Host – the infectious agent enters a person who is not resistant or immune. Control at this level is directed towards the identification of the patients at risk, treat their underlying condition for susceptibility, or isolate them from the reservoir.

MEDICAL ASEPSIS

Best defined as "the destruction of pathogenic microorganisms after they leave the body." It also involves environmental hygiene measures such as equipment cleaning and disinfection procedures. Methods of medical asepsis are Standard Precautions and Transmission-Based Precautions.

HANDWASHING

Hand washing is the most important means of preventing the spread of infection. A routine hand wash procedure uses plain soap to remove soil and transient bacterial. Hand antisepsis requires the use of antimicrobial soap to remove, kill or inhibit transient microorganisms. It is important that all healthcare personnel learn proper hand washing procedures. Foam or cream disinfectants may also be used.

BARRIER PROTECTION

Protective clothing provides a barrier against infection. Used properly, it will provide protection to the person wearing it; disposed of properly it will assist in the spread of infection. Learning how to put on and remove protective clothing is vital to insure the health and wellness of the person wearing the PPE. PPE's or personal protective equipment includes:

- Gloves. Gloves are worn for three reasons:
  - Gloves are worn to provide protective barrier and to prevent gross contamination of the hands when touching blood, body fluids, secretions, excretions, mucous membranes, and nonintact skin.
  - Gloves are worn to reduce the likelihood that microorganisms present on the hands of personnel will be transmitted to patients during invasive or other patient-care procedures that involve touching a patient's mucous membranes and nonintact skin.
  - Gloves are worn to reduce the likelihood that hands of personnel contaminated with microorganisms from a patient or a fomite can transmit these microorganisms to another patient.

- Masks
- Goggles
- Face Shields
- Respirator

A phlebotomist with a diagnosed case of Group A strep must avoid contact with patients for 24 hours after being started on an appropriate antibiotic and appearing symptom free.

ISOLATION PRECAUTIONS

For many years, the CDC recommended universal precautions, which is a method of infection control that assumed that all human blood and body fluids were potentially infectious. The CDC issued revised guidelines consisting of two tiers or levels of precautions: Standard Precautions and Transmission-Based Precautions.

STANDARD PRECAUTIONS

This is an infection control method designed to prevent direct contact with blood and other body fluids and tissues by using barrier protection and work control practices. Under the standard precautions, all patients are presumed to be infective for blood-borne pathogens. Infection control practices to be used with all patients. These replace universal precautions and body substance isolation. They are used when there is a possibility of contact with any of the following:

- Blood
- All body fluids, secretions, and excretions (except sweat), regardless of whether or not they contain visible blood
- Nonintact skin
- Mucous membranes designed to reduce the risk of transmission of microorganisms from both recognized and unrecognized sources of infections.
- OSHA requires that employers must offer the Hep B immunization series to all employees who are at risk of exposure during their normal work duties within 10 days of employment at no charge to the employee.

The standard precautions are:

- Wear gloves when collecting and handling blood, body fluids, or tissue specimen.
- Wear face shields when there is a danger for splashing on mucous membranes.
- Dispose of all needles and sharp objects in puncture-proof containers without recapping.

Transmission-Based Precautions – the second tier of precautions are to be used when the patient is known or suspected of being infected with contagious disease. They are to be used in addition to standard precautions. All types of isolation are condensed into three categories:

- *Contact precautions*: are designed to reduce the risk of transmission of microorganisms by direct or indirect contact. Direct-contact transmission involves skin-to-skin contact and physical transfer of microorganisms to a susceptible host from an infected or colonized person. Indirect-contact transmission involves contact with a contaminated intermediate object in the patient's environment.

- *Airborne precautions*: are designed to reduce the risk of airborne transmission of infectious agents. Microorganisms carried in this manner can be dispersed widely by air currents and may become inhaled by or deposited on a susceptible host within the same room or over a longer distance from the source patient. Special air handling and ventilation are required to prevent airborne transmission. Most isolation rooms have a preparation area that has negative pressure. This area is a small room that allows the medical worker to gown, glove, mask, etc in preparation for entering and exiting the room as well as disposing of contaminated objects.
- *Droplet precautions*: are designed to reduce the risk of droplet transmission of infectious agents. Droplet transmission involves contact with the conjunctivae or the mucous membranes of the nose or mouth of a susceptible person with large-particle droplets generated from the source person primarily during coughing, sneezing, or talking. Because droplets generally travel only short distances, usually three feet or less, and do not remain suspended in the air, special air handling and ventilation are not required.
- *Disinfection*: the third procedure used in medical asepsis using various chemicals that can be used to destroy many pathogenic microorganisms. Since chemicals can irritate skin and mucous membranes, they are used only on inanimate objects.

The least expensive and most readily available disinfectant for surfaces such as countertops is a 1:10 solution of household bleach. This solution should be prepared daily. Boiling water (temperature of 212 F) is considered a form of disinfection, but use of it in today's medical setting is limited to items that:

1. Will not be used in invasive procedures;

2. Will not be inserted into body orifices nor be used in a sterile procedure.

Entering and Existing the Room

- Take only the needed supplies into the room
- Leave requisitions outside the room
- Leave the tourniquet in the room
- Used needles, swabs etc. left in the room
- Any body fluid on the outside of the container is to be wiped off
- Wash hands after leaving the room
- Place all PPE in appropriate containers

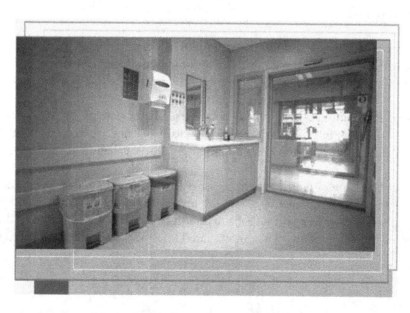

Standard Precautions (Formally Known as Universal Precautions and Introduced by the CDC)

Developed to prevent the spread of blood-borne pathogens particularly HBV and HIV

1. All health care workers routinely use appropriate barrier precautions

2. Hands and other skin surfaces should be washed immediately if contaminated with body fluids

3. Take precautions to prevent injuries from sharp instruments or devices

4. Mouth-to-mouth protection devices available

5. Health care workers who have exudation lesions or weeping dermatitis should refrain from direct patient care

6. Pregnant health care workers are not known to be at greater risk for contracting a viral infection but should strictly adhere to precautions

Antiseptics for skin are:

- 70% Ethyl alcohol
- 70% Isopropyl alcohol
- Hydrogen peroxide
- Tincture of iodine
- Benzalkonium chloride
- Hexylresorcinol

The Phlebotomy Technician Program

Student Handout #5

SAFETY AND FIRST AID

Safety hazards abound in the healthcare setting, many of which can cause serious injury or disease. The Occupational Safety and Health Administration (OSHA) is responsible for the identification of the various hazards present in the workplace and for the creation of rules and regulations to minimize exposure to such hazards. Employers are mandated to institute measures that will assure safe working conditions and health workers have the obligation to know and follow those measures.

Types of Hazards

- **Biologic:** infectious agents that can cause bacterial, viral, fungal, or parasitic infections.
- **Sharps:** needles, lancets, and broken glass can puncture and cut and cause blood-borne pathogen exposure.
- **Chemical:** preservatives and chemicals used in the laboratory. There is possible exposure to toxic, carcinogenic or caustic substances.
- **Electrical:** high-voltage equipment can cause burns and shock.
- **Fire or explosive:** Bunsen burners, oxygen and chemicals can cause burns or dismemberment.
- **Physical:** wet floors, heavy lifting can cause falls, sprains and strains.
- **Allergic reaction:** latex sensitivity that can cause allergic reactions ranging from simple dermatitis to anaphylaxis.

OSHA Standards

1. All employers and employees observe universal precautions

2. PPE devices available

3. Engineering practices controls that isolate or remove blood borne pathogen hazard

This Packet and any attachments are the confidential property of CCI and are for class purposes only – do not print

4. Work practice controls that reduce the risk of exposure

5. Appropriate cleaning method for spills

6. Hepatitis vaccine available at no cost to employees

7. Post exposure follow up for exposed employees

8. Training and educational information on blood-borne pathogens

9. Labels and signs that warn of biological hazards and contaminated waste

BLOOD-BORNE EXPOSURE PLAN

After an exposure incident, the employee must:

- Decontaminate the needle-stick site with appropriate antiseptic
- Flush exposed mucous membrane site with water for 10 minutes
- Report incident to the supervisor for follow-up care

OSHA Universal Precautions

- All patients should be assumed to be infectious for HIV and other blood-borne pathogens

EXPOSURE PROCEDURE

The medical evaluation involves the following:

- Employees blood is tested for HIV
- Source is tested for HIV and HBV and possibly for Hep. C
- If the source tests positive for HIV, the employee is counseled, evaluated for HIV and offered AZT
- If the source does not consent to testing the exposed employee is given immune globulin or an HBV vaccination
- The exposed employee is counseled to be on the alert for acute viral symptoms with 12 weeks of exposure

Safety and First Aid

- Wear gloves at all times
- Gloves must be changed between patients and hands washed
- A lab coat is to be worn over uniform and left in the lab when on break or lunch
- Mask worn to protect against TB
- Needles never recapped
- All sharps disposed of in appropriate containers
- Blood collection items disposed of appropriately
- Blood collection devices and surfaces decontaminated with 10% solution of bleach

Laboratory Safety

- Patient specimens covered at all times during transportation and centrifugation
- Centrifugation of specimens performed within biohazard safety hood

- Waste from collected specimens placed in appropriate containers
- Needles not recapped, bent or broken

Fire Safety

1. **Class A fire:** ordinary combustible material: wood, rubbish, cloth etc.

   - Use A (pressurized water) or ABC (Dry Chemical) fire extinguisher

2. **Class B fire:** vapor-air mixture such as gasoline

   - Use ABC (Dry Chemical) or BC (Carbon dioxide) fire extinguisher

3. **Class C fire:** in or near electrical equipment

   - Use BC (Carbon dioxide), Halon or ABC (Dry Chemical) fire extinguisher

4. **Class D fire:** combustible metals, magnesium, sodium, and lithium

   - Use Metal X to cover burning material with extinguishing agent

PASS = Pull, Aim, Squeeze, and Sweep

RACE = Remove, Activate, Contain, Evacuate

Electrical Safety

- Avoid using extension cords
- Do not overload circuits
- Do not use damaged cords
- Unplug equipment prior to servicing
- Do not repair equipment you are not trained for
- Do not mix electricity and water
- If electrical shock occurs – shut off electricity, call for medical assistance, initiate CPR if needed, keep victim warm

Radiation Safety

- The principles of radiation safety are distance, shielding and time

Chemical Safety

- Always wear proper PPE
- Always use proper chemical spill kits
- Never store chemicals above eye level
- Never add water to acid
- Do not indiscriminately mix chemicals together
- Always label containers
- Never pour chemicals into dirty containers
- Never use chemicals in ways they were not intended
- The agency that developed a label designed to communicate specific hazards associated with hazardous chemicals is NFPA
- Labeling hazardous material is required by OSHA's Hazardous Communication Standard

MSDS SHEETS

Must be provided to employees according to the Hazard Communication Standard (29 CFR 1910.1200) and contain the following about hazardous products on the worksite:

- Provide warning
- Explain nature of hazard
- State special precautions to eliminate risk
- Explain first aid treatment
- NFPA is responsible for the labeling system for hazardous chemicals

Patient Safety

- Dispose of all phlebotomy equipment appropriately
- Put bed rail back up if you put it down
- Report any unusual odors to the nurse
- Check for spills on the floor and arrange for clean up
- Do not touch electrical equipment while drawing blood
- Report any of the following to the nurse: red or swollen IV site, if blood is backing up into the IV line or if the IV solution is empty
  - If the patient alarm is sounding on the IV system
  - If the patient is unresponsive or in unusual pain

LATEX ALLERGY

Equipment a phlebotomist uses which may contain latex are:

- Tourniquets
- Syringes
- Gloves
- Adhesive tape

EMERGENCY PROCEDURES

The ability to recognize and react quickly to an emergency may be the difference of life or death for the patient. As patients react differently to various situations, it is important for all healthcare professionals to be prepared in an emergency.

External Hemorrhage: controlling the bleeding is most effectively accomplished by elevating the affected part above heart level and applying direct pressure to the wound. Do not attempt to elevate a broken extremity as this could cause further damage.

Shock: occurs when there is 'insufficient return of blood flow to the heart, resulting in inadequate supply of oxygen to all organs and tissues of the body.' Patients experiencing trauma may go into shock and for some patients, seeing their own blood may induce shock. Common symptoms:

- Pale, cold, clammy skin
- Rapid, weak pulse
- Increased, shallow breathing rate
- Expressionless face/staring eyes

Type Reaction	Symptoms/Signs	Cause	Prevention/Management
Irritant Contact Dermatitis	Scaling, drying, cracking of skin	Direct skin irritation by gloves, powder, soaps/detergents, incomplete hand drying	Obtain medical diagnosis, avoid irritant product, consider use of cotton glove liners, consider alternative gloves/products
Allergic Contact Dermatitis (Type IV delayed hypersensitivity or allergic contact sensitivity)	Blistering, itching, crusting (similar to poison ivy reaction)	Accelerators (e.g., thiurams, carbamates, benzothiazoles) processing chemicals (e.g., biocides, antioxidants) Consider penetration of glove barrier by chemicals	Obtain medical diagnosis, identify chemical Consider use of glove liners such as cotton Use alternative glove material without chemical Assure glove material is suitable for intended use (proper barrier)
NRL Allergy - IgE/histamine mediated (Type I immediate hypersensitivity) --------------- A) Localized contact urticaria which may be associated with or progress to: B) Generalized Reaction	-------------- Hives in area of contact with NRL -------------- Include: generalized urticaria, rhinitis, wheezing, swelling of mouth, and shortness of breath. Can progress to anaphylactic shock	NRL proteins: direct contact with or breathing NRL proteins, including glove powder containing proteins, from powdered gloves or the environment	Obtain medical diagnosis, allergy consultation, substitute non-NRL gloves for affected worker and other non-NRL products Eliminate exposure to glove powder - use of reduced protein, powder free gloves for coworkers Clean NRL-containing powder from environment Consider NRL safe environment

First Aid for Shock

- Maintain an open airway for the victim
- Call for assistance
- Keep the victim lying down with the head lower than the rest of the body
- Attempt to control bleeding or cause of shock (if known)
- Keep the victim warm until help arrives

LATEX SENSITIVITY

Latex sensitivity is an emerging and important problem in the health care field. Following the development of Universal Precaution Standards (OSHA, 1980), the use of natural rubber latex gloves for infection control skyrocketed. Within the last decade, however, the incidence of latex sensitivity has grown. Every health care worker must be concerned about latex sensitivity. Individuals with a known sensitivity to latex should wear a medical alert bracelet.

OSHA REGULATIONS

Revision to OSHA's Bloodborne Pathogens Standard
Technical Background and Summary

April 2001

BACKGROUND

The Occupational Safety and Health Administration published the Occupational Exposure to Bloodborne Pathogens standard in 1991 because of a significant health risk associated with exposure to viruses and other microorganisms that cause bloodborne diseases. Of primary concern are the human immunodeficiency virus (HIV) and the hepatitis B and hepatitis C viruses.

The standard sets forth requirements for employers with workers exposed to blood or other potentially infectious materials. In order to reduce or eliminate the hazards of occupational exposure, an employer must implement an exposure control plan for the worksite with details on employee protection measures. The plan must also describe how an employer will use a combination of engineering and work practice controls, ensure the use of personal protective clothing and equipment, provide training, medical surveillance, hepatitis B vaccinations, and signs and labels, among other provisions. Engineering controls are the primary means of eliminating or minimizing employee exposure and include the use of safer medical devices, such as needleless devices, shielded needle devices, and plastic capillary tubes.

Nearly 10 years have passed since the bloodborne pathogens standard was published. Since then, many different medical devices have been developed to reduce the risk of needlesticks and other sharps injuries. These devices replace sharps with non-needle devices or incorporate safety features designed to reduce injury. Despite these advances in technology, needlesticks and other sharps injuries continue to be of concern due to the high frequency of their occurrence and the severity of the health effects.

The Centers for Disease Control and Prevention estimate that healthcare workers sustain nearly 600,000 percutaneous injuries annually involving contaminated sharps. In response to both the continued concern over such exposures and the technological developments which can increase employee protection, Congress passed the **Needlestick Safety and Prevention Act** directing OSHA to revise the bloodborne pathogens standard to establish in greater detail requirements that employers identify and make use of effective and safer medical devices. That revision was published on Jan. 18, 2001, and became effective April 18, 2001.

SUMMARY

The revision to OSHA's bloodborne pathogens standard added new requirements for employers, including additions to the exposure control plan and keeping a sharps injury log. It does <u>not</u> impose new requirements for employers to protect workers from sharps injuries; the original standard already required employers to adopt engineering and work practice controls that would eliminate or minimize employee exposure from hazards associated with bloodborne pathogens.

The revision does, however, specify in greater detail the engineering controls, such as safer medical devices, which must be used to reduce or eliminate worker exposure.

EXPOSURE CONTROL PLAN

The revision includes new requirements regarding the employer's Exposure Control Plan, including an annual review and update to reflect changes in technology that eliminate or reduce exposure to bloodborne pathogens. The employer must:

- Take into account innovations in medical procedure and technological developments that reduce the risk of exposure (e.g., newly available medical devices designed to reduce needle-sticks); and
- Document consideration and use of appropriate, commercially available, and effective safer devices (e.g., describe the devices identified as candidates for use, the method(s) used to evaluate those devices, and justification for the eventual selection).

No one medical device is considered appropriate or effective for all circumstances. Employers must select devices that, based on reasonable judgment:

- Will not jeopardize patient or employee safety or be medically inadvisable; and
- Will make an exposure incident involving a contaminated sharp less likely to occur.

EMPLOYEE INPUT

Employers must solicit input from non-managerial employees responsible for direct patient care regarding the identification, evaluation, and selection of effective engineering controls, including safer medical devices. Employees selected should represent the range of exposure situations encountered in the workplace, such as those in geriatric, pediatric, or nuclear medicine, and others involved in direct care of patients.

OSHA will check for compliance with this provision during inspections by questioning a representative number of employees to determine if and how their input was requested.

Documentation of Employee Input

Employers are required to document, in the Exposure Control Plan, how they received input from employees. This obligation can be met by:

- Listing the employees involved and describing the process by which input was requested; or
- Presenting other documentation, including references to the minutes of meetings, copies of documents used to request employee participation, or records of responses received from employees.

RECORD KEEPING

Employers who have employees who are occupationally exposed to blood or other potentially infectious materials, and who are required to maintain a log of occupational injuries and illnesses under existing record keeping rules, must also maintain a sharps injury log. That log will be maintained in a manner that protects the privacy of employees. At a minimum, the log will contain the following:

- The type and brand of device involved in the incident;
- Location of the incident (e.g., department or work area); and
- Description of the incident

The sharps injury log may include additional information as long as an employee's privacy is protected. The employer can determine the format of the log.

MODIFICATION OF DEFINITIONS

The revision to the bloodborne pathogens standard includes modification of definitions relating to engineering controls. Two terms have been added to the standard, while the description of an existing term has been amended.

Engineering Controls

Engineering Controls include all control measures that isolate or remove a hazard from the workplace, such as sharps disposal containers and self-sheathing needles. The original bloodborne pathogens standard was not specific regarding the applicability of various engineering controls (other than the above examples) in the healthcare setting. The revision now specifies that "safer medical devices, such as sharps with engineered sharps injury protections and needleless systems" constitute an effective engineering control, and must be used where feasible.

Sharps with Engineered Sharps Injury Protections

This is a new term which includes non-needle sharps or needle devices containing built-in safety features that are used for collecting fluids or administering medications or other fluids, or other procedures involving the risk of sharps injury. This description covers a broad array of devices, including:

- Syringes with a sliding sheath that shields the attached needle after use;
- Needles that retract into a syringe after use;
- Shielded or retracting catheters
- Intravenous medication (IV) delivery systems that use a catheter port with a needle housed in a protective covering.

Needleless Systems

This is a new term defined as devices that provide an alternative to needles for various procedures to reduce the risk of injury involving contaminated sharps. Examples include:

- IV medication systems which administer medication or fluids through a catheter port using non-needle connections; and
- Jet injection systems that deliver liquid medication beneath the skin or through a muscle.

The Phlebotomy Technician Program

Student Handout #6

MEDICAL TERMINOLOGY, ANATOMY, AND PHYSIOLOGY OF ORGAN SYSTEMS

BASIC WORD STRUCTURE

Medical terms are like individual jigsaw puzzles. Once you divide the terms into their parts and learn the meaning of these parts, you can use this knowledge to understand many other medical terms. Terms can be broken down into the following parts:

1. Root – this is the main term in the word and describes the essential meaning of the word.

2. Combining vowel – this is a vowel that combines the root with the other parts of the word. In medical terms, this vowel is most commonly an "O".

3. Suffix – this is found at the end of a word.

4. Prefix – this is found at the beginning of a word.

5. Combining form – this is the root term combined with the combining vowel together.

Now let's put it all together and look at the word hematology. Let's break it down into its word parts:

HEMAT / O / LOGY

This Packet and any attachments are the confidential property of CCI and are for class purposes only – do not print

HEMAT – is the root word and in all medical terms means blood
O – the letter "O" is the combining vowel which attaches the root with the suffix
LOGY – is a suffix and in medical terms means the "study of"

Now that we know what each of these word parts represents, let's take another look at the word hematology. When reading medical terms, you read from the end of the term to the beginning of the term. In other words from back to front! First, break the term into the different parts, so in hematology, **LOGY** is the suffix, "O" is the combining vowel, and **HEMAT** is the root. Starting from back to front we see LOGY which means "study of" and then the combining vowel "O" and finally HEMAT which means "blood." Therefore the medical term **HEMATOLOGY** means the "study of blood".

Let's look at another term:

ELECTROCARDIOGRAM

First let's break it down into each word part:

ELECTR / O / CARDI / O / GRAM

Now reading from back to front:

GRAM – means "record" in all medical terms
"O" – combining vowel
CARDI – means "heart" in all medical terms
"O" – combining vowel
ELECTR – means electricity

Put all together, ELECTROCARDIOGRAM means "record of heart electricity."

COMMON MEDICAL WORD PARTS AND THEIR MEANINGS

Combining Form	Meaning
Aden/o	Gland
Arthr/o	Joint
Bi/o	Life
Carcin/o	Cancer
Cephal/o	Head
Cerebr/o	Cerebrum
Cyst/o	Urinary bladder
Cyt/o	Cell
Demat/o or Dem/o	Skin
Electr/o	Electricity
Encephal/o	Brain
Enter/o	Intestine
Erythr/o	Red
Gastr/o	Stomach
Gnos/o	Knowledge
Gynec/o	Women/Female
Hemat/o or Hem/o	Blood
Hepat/o	Liver
Lapar/o	Abdomen

This Packet and any attachments are the confidential property of CCI and are for class purposes only – do not print

Combining Form	Meaning
Leuk/o	White
Nephr/o	Kidney
Neur/o	Nerve
Onc/o	Tumor
Ophthalm/o	Eye
Oste/o	Bone
Path/o	Disease
Psych/o	Mind
Ren/o	Kidney
Rhin/o	Nose
Sarc/o	Flesh
Thromb/o	Clotting

Suffix	Meaning
-al	pertaining to
-algia	Pain
-cyte	Cell
-ectomy	Cutting out, removal, excision
-emia	Blood condition
-globin	Protein
-gram	Record
-ia	Condition
-ic	Pertaining to
-ism	condition/process
-itis	Inflammation
-logist	Specialist in the
-logy	Study of
-oma	Tumor or mass
-opsy	To view
-osis	Abnormal condition
-scope	Instrument to visually examine
-scopy	Process of visually examining
-sis	State of
-tomy	Process of cutting into

Prefix	Meaning
a-, an-	No, not
aut-	Self
dia-	Complete, through
dys-	Bad, painful, difficult, abnormal
endo-	within
exo-	Outside
hyper-	Excessive, more than normal, too much
hypo-	Below, less than normal, under
pro-	Before
re-	Back
retro-	Behind
sub-	Below, under
trans-	Across, through

THE HUMAN BODY

The human body is studied using these guides:

- **Anatomy:** the study of the structural components of the body
- **Physiology:** the study of the functional components of the body
- **Pathology:** the study of all aspects of disease and abnormal conditions of the body

SURFACE REGIONS OF THE BODY

Front or anterior/ventral body plane:

- Thoracic cavity
- Abdominal cavity
- Pelvic cavity

SURFACE REGIONS OF THE HUMAN BODIES

Back or posterior, or dorsal surface is divided into:

- Cranial cavity
- Spinal cavity

Planes of the Body

- **Sagittal Plane:** runs lengthwise from front to back dividing the body into a left and right half
- **Frontal Plane:** runs lengthwise from side to side dividing the body into anterior and posterior sections
- **Transverse Plane:** runs horizontally, dividing the body into upper and lower sections

Medial/Lateral

- **Medial** refers to: towards the mid-line
- **Lateral** refers to: towards the sides of the body

STRUCTURAL ORGANIZATION

The human body can be divided into 8 structural levels:

- atoms
- molecules (chemical constituents)
- small structures within cells
- cells
- tissues
- organs
- organ systems
- organism (human body)

Medical Regions of the Human Body

- Head and neck
- Upper torso
- Lower torso
- Back
- Arms
- Legs
- Hands and feet

The Human Cell

- **Nucleus:** control mechanism that governs the function of the individual cell (growth, repair, reproduction, and metabolism). If nucleus is damaged, the cell will die. RBC's lose their nucleus when they mature
- **Nucleolus:** aids in metabolism and reproduction
- **Cytoplasm:** contains mostly water and fills up the rest of the cell membrane
- **Mitochondria:** produces energy for cells
- **Ribosomes:** assembles amino acids into proteins
- **Endoplasmic reticulum:** transport channel between cell and nuclear membranes
- **Lysosomes:** release digestive enzymes for digestion of food particles
- **Golgi apparatus:** stores protein
- **Centriole:** plays a role in cell division

Common Terms

- **Deoxyribonucleic acid (DNA):** a long molecule containing thousands of genes
- **Homeostasis:** a condition in which the human body strives for a steady normal, healthy condition
- **Metabolism:** the breaking down of chemical substances to use energy
- **Catabolism:** series of chemical reactions in the cell to change complex substances into simpler ones and releasing energy
- **Anabolism:** process by which cells use energy to make complex compounds from simpler ones

MAJOR ORGAN SYSTEMS

Integumentary System

Consists of

- skin, sweat, and oil glands
- hair
- fingernails
- teeth

Functions

- protects underlying tissues
- regulates body temperature
- eliminates some wastes
- receives sensory stimuli: touch, pressure, temperature, pain
- prevents water loss

Common Disorders

- acne
- burns
- carcinoma
- fungal infections, impetigo
- keloid
- pediculosis
- puritis
- psoriasis
- dermatitis – inflammation of the dermis

Diagnostic Tests

- Biopsies
- KOH prep
- Microbiological cultures
- Tissue cultures

SKELETAL SYSTEM

Components

- Bones
- Cartilage
- Tendons
- Ligaments
- Joints

Functions

- Provides Support
- Protects Organs
- Stores Minerals
- Allows Leverage and Movement
- Produces Blood Cells (hemopoiesis)
- Periosteum – covers bone and contains blood vessels to transport blood from inside the bone to outside layers

Disorders

- Arthritis
- Bursitis
- Gout
- Osteomyelitis
- Osteoporosis
- Rickets
- Tumors

Diagnostic Tests

- Alkaline Phosphatase (Alp)
- Calcium
- Cubic
- ESR
- Phosphorus
- Uric Acid
- Vitamin D

MUSCULAR SYSTEM

Components

- Skeletal Muscles
- Cardiac Muscle (Heart)
- Smooth Muscles (Walls of Hollow Organs)

Functions

- Permits Movement
- Produces Heat
- Maintains Posture

Disorders

- Atrophy
- Muscular Dystrophy (MD)
- Myalgia
- Tendinitis

Diagnostic Tests

- Autoimmune Antibodies
- Ck Isoenzymes
- Creatinine Phosphokinase (CPK)
- Lactate Dehydrogenase (LDH)
- Lactic Acid
- Myoglobin

NERVOUS SYSTEM

Diagnostic Tests

- Brain
- Spinal Cord
- Nerves
- Sense Organs: Eyes, Ears, Tongue, and Sensory Receptors in the Skin

Functions

- Allows Communication throughout the body and regulates body functions
- Detects Sensations
- Controls Movement and Physiological Functions
- Controls Intellectual Processes

Disorders

- ALS
- Encephalitis
- Epilepsy
- Hydrocephaly
- Meningitis
- MS

Disorders

- Neuralgia
- Parkinson's disease
- Shingles

Diagnostic Tests

- Acetykcholine Receptor Antibody
- Cerebral Spinal Fluid Analysis
- Cholinesterase
- Drug Levels – would need to work with pharmacy to monitor

RESPIRATORY SYSTEM

Components

- Nasal Cavity
- Pharynx
- Larynx
- Trachea
- Bronchi
- Lungs

Functions

- Filters Air, Exchanges Gases
- Supplies Oxygen and Removes Carbon Dioxide
- Helps Regulate Blood pH
- Protects Vocal Cords
- Inhalation – oxygen is exchanged for carbon dioxide
- Exhalation – carbon dioxide released outside

Disorders

- Asthma
- Bronchitis
- Cystic Fibrosis
- Respiratory Distress Syndrome
- Respiratory Syncytial Virus
- Respiratory Tract Infections

- Emphysema
- Pleurisy
- Pneumonia

- Rhinitis
- Tonsillitis
- Tuberculosis

Diagnostic Tests

- Alkaline Phosphatase (Alp)
- Arterial Blood Gases
- Complete Blood Cell Count (Cubic)
- Bronchial Washings
- Drug Levels
- Tuberculin Skin Test

- Electrolytes
- Microbiological Cultures
- Pleuralcentesis
- Sputum Cultures

DIGESTIVE SYSTEM

Components

- Mouth
- Salivary Glands
- Esophagus
- Stomach
- Intestines

- Liver and Gall Bladder
- Pancreas
- Teeth
- Appendix
- Pharynx

Functions

- Breaks Down Food Physically and Chemically
- Absorbs Nutrients
- Removes Solid Waste

Disorders

- Cancer
- Parasitic Infections

- Polyps
- Ulcers

Diagnostic Tests

- Occult Blood Test

- Ova and Parasite Analysis

URINARY SYSTEM

Components

- Kidneys
- Ureters

- Bladder
- Urethra

Functions

- Filters Blood to Eliminate Waste
- Helps Maintain Blood pH

- Regulates Water Balance

Disorders

- Cystitis
- Kidney Stones
- Nephritis
- Renal Failure
- Uremia
- Urinary Tract Infection

Diagnostic Tests

- Albumin
- Ammonia
- Blood Urea Nitrogen (Bun)
- Creatinine Clearance
- Electrolytes
- Osmolality
- Urinalysis
- Urine Cultures

REPRODUCTIVE SYSTEM

Components

- **Male**: Testes, Penis, Duct System, Glands
- **Female**: Ovaries, Uterine Tubes, Uterus, Vagina, External Genitalia
- **Accessory Organs**: Mammary Glands

Functions

- Secretes Hormones
- Produces Germ Cells for Reproduction (Sperm and Ova)
- In The Female, Maintains Fetus and Produces Milk for Nourishment of Neonate

Disorders

- Cervical, Ovarian, Uterine Cancer
- Infertility
- Ovarian Cyst
- Prostate, Testicular Cancer
- Sexually Transmitted Diseases (STDs)

Diagnostic Tests

- Acid Phosphatase
- Estrogen
- Follicle-Stimulating Hormone (FSH)
- Human Chorionic Gonadotropin (HCG)
- Luteinizing Hormone (LH)
- Microbiological Cultures
- Pap Smear
- Rapid Plasma Reagin (RPR)
- Testosterone
- Tissue Analysis

ENDOCRINE SYSTEM

- The Human Body Has Two Types Of Glands:
  - Exocrine Glands: Secrete Fluids Such As Sweat, Saliva, Mucus, And Digestive Juices
  - Endocrine Glands: Ductless Glands That Secrete Hormones Directly Into The Bloodstream
- This Glandular System Has The Same Function As The Nervous System:
- Communication
- Control
- Integration

Components

- **Hormone-Producing Structures:** Pituitary, Pineal, Thyroid, Parathyroid, Thymus, and Adrenal Glands
- Ovaries, Testes, and Pancreas

Functions

- Composes a Communications System that uses Hormones as Chemical Messengers
- Helps Maintain Homeostasis
- Regulates Body Activities, such as Metabolism and Reproduction

Disorders

- Acromegaly
- Addison's Disease
- Cretinism
- Cushing's Syndrome
- Diabetes Insipidus
- Diabetes Mellitus
- Dwarfism
- Gigantism
- Goiter
- Hyperinsulism
- Hypoglycemia
- Hypo- And Hyperthyroidism

Diagnostic Tests

- Adrenocorticotropic Hormone (ACTH)
- Aldosterone
- Antidiuretic Hormone (ADH)
- Cortisol
- Erythropoietin
- Glucagon
- Glucose Tolerance Tests (GTT's)
- Growth Hormone (GH)
- Insulin
- Rennin
- Serotonin
- Thyroid Function: T3, T4, TSH

LYMPHATIC SYSTEM

Components

- Lymph Vessels And Nodes
- Spleen
- Thymus Gland
- Tonsils
- Bone Marrow

Functions

- Maintains Tissue Fluid Balance
- Filters Blood And Lymph
- Produces WBC's To Protect Body From Disease
- Absorbs Fats

Disorders

- Immune Disorders
- Infection Processes
- Tumors (Lymphoma, Hodgkin's Disease)

Diagnostic Tests

- Bone Marrow Analysis
- Cell Surface Markers

The Phlebotomy Technician Program

Student Handout #7

THE CARDIOVASCULAR AND LYMPHATIC SYSTEMS

THE CIRCULATORY SYSTEM

The function of this system is to deliver oxygen, nutrients, hormones, and enzymes to the cells (exchange is done at the capillary level) and to transport cellular waste such as carbon dioxide and urea to the organs (lung and kidneys, respectively) where they can be expelled from the body. It is a transport system where the blood is the vehicle; the blood vessels, the tubes, and the heart work as the pump.

THE HEART

The heart acts as two pumps in series (right and left sides), connected by two circulations, with each pump equipped with two valves, the function of which is to maintain a one-way flow of blood. The two circulations are:

- **Pulmonary circulation** – this carries deoxygenated blood from the right ventricle to the lungs (oxygenation takes place at the alveoli) and returns oxygenated blood from the lungs to the left atrium.
- **Systemic circulation** – this carries oxygenated blood from the left ventricle throughout the body.

Each side of the heart (right and left) is composed of an upper chamber, the atrium, and a lower chamber, the ventricle. The right side has two valves:

- **The tricuspid valve** – this is an atrioventricular valve, being situated between the right atrium and right ventricle.
- **The pulmonic valve** – a semi lunar valve situated between the right ventricle and the pulmonary artery.

The left side also has two valves:

- **The mitral valve** (also known as the bicuspid valve) – this is another atrioventricular valve, being situated between the left atrium and left ventricle.
- **The aortic valve** – a semi lunar valve situated between the left ventricle and the aorta.

The heart has three layers:

Endocardium – the endothelial inner layer lining of the heart.
Myocardium – the muscular middle layer. This is the contractile element of the heart.
Epicardium – the fibrous outer layer of the heart. The coronary arteries, which supply blood to the heart, are found in this layer.

THE BLOOD VESSELS

The blood vessels are: aorta, arteries, arterioles, capillaries, venules, veins, superior and inferior vena cavae.

The blood vessels, except for the capillaries, are composed of three layers. The outer connective tissue layer is called the tunica adventitia. The middle smooth muscle layer is called the tunica media. The inner endothelial layer is called the tunica intima.

The aorta, arteries, and arterioles carry oxygenated blood from the heart to the various parts of the body; while the venules, veins and the superior and inferior vena cavae carry deoxygenated blood back to the heart.

The capillaries, composed only of a layer of endothelial cells, connect the arterioles and venules. As such, capillary blood is a mixture of arterial and venous blood. The thin walls allow rapid exchange of oxygen, carbon dioxide, nutrients and waste products between the blood and tissue cells.

BLOOD

The average adult has 5 to 6 liters of blood. It is composed of a liquid portion called the 'plasma', and a cellular portion called the 'formed elements'. Plasma comprises 55% of the circulating blood and it contains proteins, amino acids, gases, electrolytes, sugars, hormones, minerals, vitamins, and water (92%). It also contains waste products such as urea that are destined for excretion.

The formed elements constitute the remaining 45% of the blood. They are **erythrocytes** (red blood cells), which comprise 99% of the formed elements, the leukocytes (white blood cells) and the **thrombocytes** (platelets). All blood cells normally originate from stem cells in the bone marrow.

The **erythrocytes** (red blood cells) contain hemoglobin, the oxygen-carrying protein. It enters the blood as an immature reticulocyte where in one to two days, it matures into an erythrocyte. There are 4.2 to 6.2 million RBC's (red blood cells) per microliter of blood. The normal life span of an RBC is 120 days.

The **leukocytes'** (white blood cells) function is to provide the body protection against infection. The normal amount of WBC's (white blood cells) for an adult is 5,000 to 10,000 per microliter. Leukocytosis, which is an increase in WBCs, is seen in cases of infection and leukemia. Leukopenia, which is a decrease in WBCs, is seen with viral infection or chemotherapy.

There are five types of WBCs in the blood. A differential count determines the percentage of each type:

1. **Neutrophils** – the most numerous, comprise about 40% to 60% of WBC population. They are phagocytic cells, meaning they engulf and digest bacteria. Their number increases in bacterial infection, and often, are the first one on the scene.

2. **Lymphocytes** – the second most numerous, comprising about 20% to 40% of the WBC population. Their number increases in viral infection, and they play a role in immunity.

3. **Monocytes** – comprising 3% to 8% of the population, they are also the largest WBCs. They are monocytes while in the circulating blood, but when they pass into the tissues, they transform into macrophages and become powerful phagocytes. Their number increases in intracellular infections and tuberculosis.

4. **Eosinophils** – represent 1% to 3% of the WBC population. They are active against antibody-labeled foreign molecules. Their numbers are increased in allergies, skin infections, and parasitic infections.

5. **Basophils** – account for 0% to 1% of WBCs in the blood. They carry histamine, which is released in allergic reactions.

The **thrombocytes** (platelets) are small irregularly shaped packets of cytoplasm formed in the bone marrow from megakaryocytes. Essential for blood coagulation, the average number of platelets is 140,000 to 440,000 per micro liter of blood. They have a life span of 9 to 12 days.

HEMOSTASIS

Hemostasis is the process by which blood vessels are repaired after injury. This process starts from vascular contraction as an initial reaction to injury, then to clot formation, and finally removal of the clot when the repair to injury is done. It occurs in four stages:

Stage 1 – Vascular phase
Injury to a blood vessel causes it to constrict slowing the flow of blood.

Stage 2 – Platelet phase
Injury to the endothelial lining causes platelets to adhere to it.

Additional platelets stick to the site finally forming a temporary platelet plug in a process called 'aggregation'. Vascular phase and platelet phase comprise the primary hemostasis. Bleeding time test is used to evaluate primary hemostasis.

Stage 3 – Coagulation phase
This involves a cascade of interactions of coagulation factors that converts the temporary platelet plug to a stable fibrin clot. The coagulation cascade involves an intrinsic system and extrinsic system, which ultimately come together in a common pathway. Activated partial thromboplastin time (APTT) – test used to evaluate the intrinsic pathway. This is also used to monitor heparin therapy. Prothrombin time (PT) – test used to evaluate the extrinsic pathway. This is also used to monitor coumadin therapy.

Stage 4 – Fibrinolysis

This is the breakdown and removal of the clot. As tissue repair starts, plasmin (an enzyme) starts breaking down the fibrin in the clot. Fibrin degradation products (FDPs) measurement is used to monitor the rate of fibrinolysis.

Blood Type

- Red Blood Cells With A Antigens Are Type A
- Cells With B Antigens Are Type B
- RBC's Containing Both A and B Antigens Are Type AB
- RBC With Neither Type A Or B Antigens Are Type O

Leukocytes

- White Blood Cells Are Divided Into Two Major Groups:
  - Granular – Granules In The Cytoplasm
  - Agranular – Without Cytoplasmic Granules
- White Blood Cells Form In The:
  - Bone Marrow
  - Lymphatic Tissues
- Granulocytes fight bacterial infection and are called neutrophilic segmented cells
- Granulocytes that function in antibody production are called lymphocytes

Thrombocytes or Platelets

- Platelets Help in The Clotting Process
- Common Laboratory Testing For Platelet Abnormalities Are:
  - Bleeding Time Test
  - Platelet Count
- The three components of coagulation are blood vessels, coagulation factors and platelets
- The intrinsic pathway is initiated through the activation of Factor XII
- Extrinsic pathways are initiated by the release of tissue thromboplastin
- The common pathway is initiated by the intrinsic and extrinsic pathways
- Fibrin degradation products are the end result of the fibrinilytic pathway

Plasma

- The liquid portion of the blood
- Composed of 90% water and 10% dissolved solutes
- The fluid plasma portion of the blood is straw colored

Buffy Coat

- The WBC's and platelets form a thin white layer above the RBC's called the buffy coat

Serum

- Serum contains essentially the same chemical constitutes as plasma, except the clotting factors and the blood cells are contained within the fibrin clot. It usually takes 30 to 60 minutes for a serum to clot without additives.

The Heart

- The human heart is a muscular organ about the size of a man's fist
- The heart contains four chambers and is located slightly to the left of the sternum
- The two atria are separated by the interatrial septum (wall)
- The interventricular septum divides the two ventricles
- The superior vena cava brings blood from the head, neck, arms and chest
- The inferior vena cava carries oxygen poor blood from the rest of the trunk and legs

Blood Circulation

- The right atrium receives blood from two large veins called the inferior and superior vena cava
- Once the blood enters the right atrium, it passes through the tricuspid valve into the right ventricle
- From the right ventricle, the blood enters the right and left pulmonary arteries
- The right and left pulmonary arteries branch into smaller arterioles and capillaries in the lungs where the exchange of carbon dioxide and oxygen takes place
- The blood then flows into the right and left pulmonary veins into the left atrium
- From the left atrium the blood flows through the bicuspid valve or the mitral valve into the left ventricle
- Blood then passes through the aortic semilunar valve into the body to distribute the nutrients and oxygen as well as pick up the carbon dioxide

Blood Pressure

- During blood circulation, pressure from the heart contracting is not only forcing the blood through the vessels but it is also placing pressure on the inside of the vessel walls
- When blood pressure is measured, the systolic pressure is the amount of pressure placed on the vessel walls when the heart contracts
- The diastolic pressure represents the amount of pressure placed on the walls of the vessels when the heart is at rest between contraction
- The average "normal" blood pressure is 120/80
- 120 is the systolic pressure
- 80 is the diastolic pressure

VESSELS AND CIRCULATION

Three types of vessels exist in the body:

- **Arteries** – carry highly oxygenated blood away from the heart
- Arteries have the largest tunica media
- **Veins** – carry deoxygenated blood back to the heart and lungs except in the pulmonary veins which carry oxygenated blood
- **Capillaries** – microscopic vessels that link the arterioles and venules

COMMON VENIPUNCTURE VEINS

The preferred site for venipuncture is the antecubital fossa of the upper extremities. The vein should be large enough to receive the shaft of the needle, and it should be visible or palpable after tourniquet placement.

Three major veins are located in the antecubital fossa, and they are:

A. **Median cubital vein** – the vein of choice because it is large and does not tend to move when the needle is inserted.
B. **Cephalic vein** – the second choice. It is usually more difficult to locate and has a tendency to move, however, it is often the only vein that can be palpated in the obese patient.
C. **Basilic vein** – the third choice. It is the least firmly anchored and located near the brachial artery. If the needle is inserted too deep, this artery may be punctured.

Cardiovascular Disorders/Diseases

- **Anemia** – anemia is a common blood disorder characterized by a decrease in the amount of red blood cells, or a decrease in the capacity of red blood cells to transport oxygen
- **Aneurysm** – an aneurysm is a swelling that occurs in an artery or vein when its wall is weakened.
- **Angina** – angina is a crushing pain or feeling of discomfort in the chest, due to inadequate oxygen supply to the heart caused by narrowing of the coronary arteries. Most angina medicines and treatments for angina either make the heart pump more slowly or improve blood flow to the heart.
- **Cardiomyopathy** – cardiomyopathy is a condition that damages the muscular wall of the lower chambers of the heart.
- **Congenital heart defects** – while some congenital heart defects are serious, many produce no problems throughout life.
- **Coronary arteries** – the coronary arteries supply the heart muscle with oxygen so that it can work. If these vessels become narrowed, angina can result. Coronary artery surgery can help relieve angina symptoms and help prevent heart attacks.
- **Diabetes** – people with diabetes are often unaware that they may have narrowed blood vessels in the heart until they block completely, causing a heart attack.
- **Heart attack** – a heart attack (myocardial infarction) occurs when the arterial blood supply to the heart muscle is blocked.
- **Heart failure** – heart failure means the heart has a reduced ability to pump blood around the body.
- **Heart murmurs** – heart murmurs are heard between heartbeats if the blood flow through the heart becomes turbulent.
- **Kawasaki disease** – Kawasaki disease is an illness in which there is inflammation of the blood vessels (vasculitis).
- **Leukemia** – a cancer of the blood-forming tissues characterized by a large increase in the numbers of white blood cells (leukocytes) in the circulation or bone marrow
- **Long QT syndrome** – an electrical problem in the heart can cause a very fast heart beat and sudden death.
- **Metabolic syndrome** – a condition that increases your risk of heart disease, stroke and diabetes.
- **Palpitations** – palpitations are sensations of excessively strong and/or irregular heartbeats. Find out more about the causes and treatment for palpitations.
- **Polycythaemia** – polycythaemia happens when there are too many red blood cells in the circulating blood.
- **Reynaud's disease** – for people who have Reynaud's disease, cold hands and feet can be a problem with serious circulation consequences.
- **Sickle Cell Anemia** – when hemoglobin of the type A becomes infected they turn into a kind of peculiar shape

Anatomy of the Heart

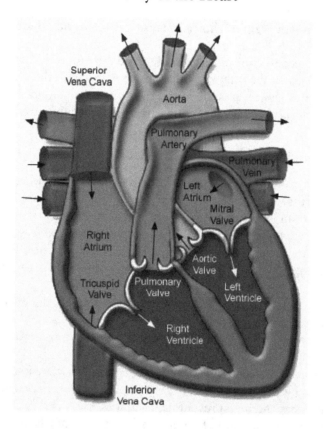

Circulatory System

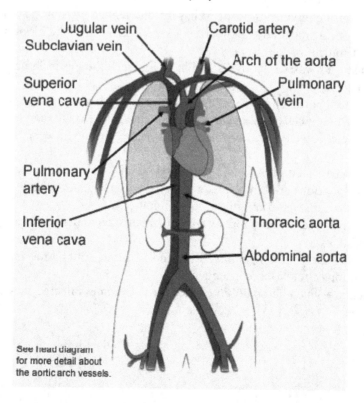

The Phlebotomy Technician Program

Student Handout #8

BLOOD COLLECTION EQUIPMENT

Vacuum Tube System

- This system required three main parts:
  - Evacuated sample tube
  - The double pointed needle
  - A special plastic holder called an adapter
- Each vacuum tube is color coded according to the additive contained within the tube
- Many tubes are designed to use directly with chemistry, hematology or microbiology instrumentation
- This system is a closed system that prevents blood from flowing outside the tube
- Blood can also be drawn into a syringe and then transferred into the vacutainer tube
- If an additive is in a tube, the blood must be inverted several times to mix the two together
- Each tube has an expiration date and stock must be rotated to prevent the use of expired tubes

Safety

- Safety-lok needle holder – this device has a protective shield that can slide over the needle
- SIMS venipuncture needle pro – this is a single use needle that allows the user to shield the needle by pressing the needle guard against a hard surface so that the guard closed over the needle

TYPES OF ADDITIVES

Anticoagulants

- prevent the blood from clotting in the tube
- heparinized whole blood is used in STAT situations
- anticoagulants often contain preservatives that can extend the metabolism and life span of the RBC's
- coagulation of blood can be prevented by the addition of oxalates, citrates, ethylenediamine tetra-acetic acid (EDTA), or heparin

Serum Separator Tubes

- These tubes contain a polymer barrier that is present in the bottom of the tube. During centrifugation, the barrier moves upwards to form a solid barrier separating the serum from the fibrin and cells
- The most common terms used to name the various tubes are:
  - SST (yellow top for H.H.) – this tube contains a serum separator and is mainly used in chemistry testing on the serum
  - Red top – this tube contains no additive and is used mainly for specialized testing or blood typing

Plasma Separator Tubes

- These tubes are used to obtain and separate a plasma sample
- These tubes contain 17 IU/ml of Lithium Heparin to prevent coagulation of the specimen
- The tubes contain an acrylic gel that forms a barrier between the cells and the plasma during centrifugation
- Light green – contains gel and lithium heparin – used for STAT and routine chemistry

Whole Blood or Plasma Specimen

- **Purple top, lavender tube** – contains EDTA—used for most hematology testing—additive bind calcium
- **Blue tops** – contain sodium citrate, mainly used in coagulation testing. **Tubes must be full for correct dilution ratio. These need to be a 9:1 ratio of blood to anticoagulant or this will adversely affect testing and patient care. This tube is one of the most rejected tubes in the laboratory due to improper filling.**
- **Gray tops** – contain sodium fluoride or lithium. This type of tube is mainly used for glycolytic inhibition testing
- **Green tops** – contain various heparin additives. Mainly used for chemistry testing.
- **Sodium heparin** – neutralizes thrombin and produces artifact residue on blood smears stained with Wright's Stain
- **Royal blue tops** – are manufactured with the lowest level of trace elements
- **Tan top tubes** – are manufactured with the lowest level of lead

Butterfly Collection Set

- comes in 21, 23 and 25 gauge needles
- mainly used for geriatric, cancer and pediatric patients
- needle attached to plastic wings to hold during insertion. Wings attached to tubing which allows maneuverability and less vacuum on the vessel. Luer at end of tubing allows addition of adapter

Needles

- The larger the gauge, the smaller the needle. The most common gauge needles used today are:
  - 21 gauge – usually used on an adult
  - 22 gauge – can be used on an adult or an adolescent
  - 23 or 25 gauge – used on a difficult draw, young child or an infant

Other Equipment

- sharps containers
- tourniquets
- gloves
- antiseptics
- gauze
- bandages
- lancets
- collection trays

COLLECTION TUBES FOR PHLEBOTOMY

Red Top	7 ml
ADDITIVE	None
MODE OF ACTION	Blood clots, and the serum is separated by centrifugation
USES	Chemistries, Immunology and Serology, Blood Bank (Cross match)

Gold Top	7 ml
ADDITIVE	Clot activator – Invert five times
MODE OF ACTION	Serum separator tube (SST) contains a gel at the bottom to separate blood from serum on centrifugation
USES	Chemistries, Immunology and Serology

Light Green Top	7 ml
ADDITIVE	Plasma Separating Tube (PST) with Lithium heparin
MODE OF ACTION	Anticoagulants with lithium heparin; Plasma is separated with PST gel at the bottom of the tube
USES	Chemistries

Red-Gray Top	7 ml
ADDITIVE	Serum Separating Tube (SST) with clot activator
MODE OF ACTION	Forms clot quickly and separates the serum with SST gel at the bottom of the tube
USES	Chemistries

Purple Top	5 ml
ADDITIVE	EDTA liquid
MODE OF ACTION	Forms calcium salts to remove calcium
USES	Hematology (CBC) and Blood Bank (Cross match); requires **full draw** – invert 8 times to prevent clotting and platelet clumping

Light Blue Top	5 ml
ADDITIVE	Buffered Sodium citrate
MODE OF ACTION	Forms calcium salts to remove calcium
USES	Coagulation tests (protime and prothrombin time), **full draw** required

Green Top	7 ml
ADDITIVE	Sodium heparin or lithium heparin
MODE OF ACTION	Inactivates thrombin and thromboplastin
USES	For lithium level, use sodium heparin. For ammonia level, use sodium or lithium heparin

Dark Blue Top	7 ml
ADDITIVE	Clot activator (Royal Blue) Sodium EDTA (Dark Blue)
MODE OF ACTION	Tube is designed to contain no contaminating metals
USES	Trace element testing (zinc, copper, lead, mercury) and toxicology

Light Gray Top	7 ml
ADDITIVE	Sodium fluoride and potassium oxalate
MODE OF ACTION	Antiglycolytic agent preserves glucose up to 5 days
USES	For lithium level, use sodium heparin Glucoses, requires **full draw** (may cause hemolysis if short draw)

Yellow Top	*[tube illustration, 7 ml]*
ADDITIVE	ACD (acid-citrate-dextrose)
MODE OF ACTION	Complement inactivation
USES	HLA tissue typing, paternity testing, DNA studies

Yellow - Black Top	*[tube illustration, 10 ml]*
ADDITIVE	Broth mixture
MODE OF ACTION	Preserves viability of microorganisms
USES	Microbiology – aerobes, anaerobes, fungi

Black Top	*[tube illustration, 7 ml]*
ADDITIVE	Sodium citrate (buffered)
MODE OF ACTION	Forms calcium salts to remove calcium
USES	Westergren Sedimentation Rate; requires **full draw**

Orange Top	*[tube illustration, 7 ml]*
ADDITIVE	Thrombin
MODE OF ACTION	Quickly clots blood
USES	STAT serum chemistries

Brown Top	*[tube illustration, 7 ml]*
ADDITIVE	Sodium heparin
MODE OF ACTION	Inactivates thrombin and thromboplastin
USES	Serum lead determination

The Phlebotomy Technician Program

Student Handout #9

PRE-ANALYTICAL COMPLICATIONS CAUSING MEDICAL ERRORS IN BLOOD COLLECTION

To Prevent a Hematoma

- Puncture only the uppermost wall of the vein
- Remove the tourniquet before removing the needle
- Use the major superficial veins
- Make sure the needle fully penetrates the uppermost wall of the vein. (Partial penetration may allow blood to leak into the soft tissue surrounding the vein by way of the needle bevel)
- Apply pressure to the venipuncture site

To Prevent Hemolysis (Which can Interfere with Many Tests)

- Mix tubes with anticoagulant additives gently 5–10 times
- Avoid drawing blood from a hematoma
- Avoid drawing the plunger back too forcefully, if using a needle and syringe, and avoid frothing of the sample
- Make sure the venipuncture site is dry
- Avoid a probing, traumatic venipuncture

Indwelling Lines or Catheters

- Potential source of test error
- Most lines are flushed with a solution of heparin to reduce the risk of thrombosis
- Discard a sample at least three times the volume of the line before a specimen is obtained for analysis

Hemoconcentration

An increased concentration of larger molecules and formed elements in the blood may be due to several factors:

- Prolonged tourniquet application (no more than 2 minutes)
- Massaging, squeezing, or probing a site
- Long-term IV therapy
- Sclerosed or occluded veins

Prolonged Tourniquet Application

- Primary effect is hemoconcentration of non-filterable elements (i.e. proteins). The hydrostatic pressure causes some water and filterable elements to leave the extracellular space
- Significant increases can be found in total protein, aspartate aminotransferase (AST), total lipids, cholesterol, iron
- Affects packed cell volume and other cellular elements

Patient Preparation Factors

- Therapeutic Drug Monitoring: different pharmacologic agents have patterns of administration, body distribution, metabolism, and elimination that affect the drug concentration as measured in the blood. Many drugs will have "peak" and "trough" levels that vary according to dosage levels and intervals. Check for timing instructions for drawing the appropriate samples.
- Effects of Exercise: Muscular activity has both transient and longer lasting effects. The creatinine kinase (CK), aspartate aminotransferase (AST), lactate dehydrogenase (LDH), and platelet count may increase.
- Stress: May cause transient elevation in white blood cells (WBC's) and elevated adrenal hormone values (cortisol and catecholamines). Anxiety that results in hyperventilation may cause acid-base imbalances, and increased lactate.
- Diurnal Rhythms: Diurnal rhythms are body fluid and analyte fluctuations during the day. For example, serum cortisol levels are highest in early morning but are decreased in the afternoon. Serum iron levels tend to drop during the day. You must check the timing of these variations for the desired collection point.
- Posture: Postural changes (supine to sitting etc.) are known to vary lab results of some analytes. Certain larger molecules are not filterable into the tissue; therefore they are more concentrated in the blood. Enzymes, proteins, lipids, iron, and calcium are significantly increased with changes in position.
- Other Factors: Age, gender, and pregnancy have an influence on laboratory testing. Normal reference ranges are often noted according to age.

Specimen Rejection

- Discrepancies between requisition forms and labeled tubes
- unlabeled tubes

- QNS
- hemolyzed specimen
- drawn in wrong tube
- improperly transported
- anticoag tube clotted
- Use of expired equipment
- contaminated specimens
- a timed specimen drawn at wrong time
- MisID
- According to CLSI, draw volumes of evacuated tubes must be within +/- 10% of the scheduled draw
- If a phlebotomist is scheduled to draw 7 mL of specimen, CLSI states that an accepted drawn volume is 6.3 to 7.7 mL

Complications in Blood Collection

- **Fainting (Syncope):** never draw a patient standing up
- **Failure to Draw Blood:** a phlebotomist is allowed 2 tries and then must request assistance
- **Excessive Bleeding:** apply pressure until the bleeding stops; if longer than five minutes, alert nurse.
- **Neurological Complications:** seizure or accidentally hitting a nerve with the needle, report these incidents
- **Mastectomy:** cannot draw blood from this side. Use back of hand or fingers if double mastectomy.
- **Vomiting:** alert nurse.
- **Iodine** – if the puncture site is prepared with providone iodine, you may see an elevation in the potassium level
- **Hematoma:** The most common complication of phlebotomy procedure. This indicates that blood has accumulated in the tissue surrounding the vein. The two most common causes are the needle going through the vein, and/or failure to apply enough pressure on the site after needle withdrawal
- **Hemoconcentration:** The increase in proportion of formed elements to plasma caused by the tourniquet being left on too long. (More than two (2) minutes)
- **Phlebitis:** Inflammation of a vein as a result of repeated venipuncture on that vein.
- **Petechiae:** These are tiny non-raised red spots that appear on the skin from rupturing of the capillaries due to the tourniquet being left on too long or too tight.
- **Thrombus:** This is a blood clot usually a consequence of insufficient pressure applied after the withdrawal of the needle.
- **Thrombophlebitis:** Inflammation of a vein with formation of a clot.
- **Septicemia:** This is a systemic infection associated with the presence of pathogenic organism introduced during a venipuncture.
- **Trauma:** This is an injury to underlying tissues caused by probing.
- **Nerve complications:** This is hitting a nerve below the vein when inserting the needle. When this happens, the patient will feel a sharp, electric tingling (and painful) sensation that radiates down the nerve into the hand. The tourniquet should be released immediately, the needle removed, and pressure held over the collection site. The incident should be reported to a supervisor and the institute's policy followed.
- **Inadvertent arterial puncture:** This occurs when the needle is inserted too deeply into the tissue. This is determined by the fact that the blood will "pulse" into the tube instead of flowing naturally.

Factors to Consider Prior to Performing the Procedure

- **Fasting** – some tests such as those for glucose, cholesterol, and triglycerides require that the patient abstain from eating for at least 12 hours. The phlebotomist must ascertain that the patient is indeed in a fasting state prior to the testing.
- **Edema** – is the accumulation of fluid in the tissues. Collection from edematous tissue alters test results.
- **Fistula** – is the permanent surgical connection between an artery and a vein. Fistulas are used for dialysis procedures and must never be used for venipunctures due to the possibility of infection.

TROUBLESHOOTING GUIDELINES

Failure to Obtain Blood

Most venipunctures are routine, but in some instances, complications can arise resulting in failure to obtain blood. The following are some of the common causes:

- The tube has lost its vacuum. This is may be due to:
  - A manufacturing defect
  - Expired tube
  - A very fine crack in the tube
- Improperly positioned needle. In many instances, slight movement of the needle can correct this.
  - The bevel of the needle is resting against the wall of the vein. Slightly rotate the needle.
  - The needle is not fully in the vein. Slowly advance the needle.
  - The needle has passed through the vein. Slowly pull back on the vein.
  - The vein was missed completely. With a gloved finger, gently determine the positions of the vein and the needle, and redirect the needle.
- Collapsed vein. This may be due to excessive pull from the vacuum tube; use of a smaller vacuum tube may remedy the situation. If it does not, remove the tourniquet, withdraw the needle, and select another vein preferably using either a syringe or butterfly.

If an Incomplete Collection or No Blood Is Obtained

- Change the position of the needle. Move it forward (it may not be in the lumen).

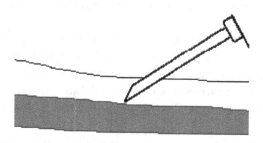

- or move it backward (it may have penetrated too far).

- Adjust the angle (the bevel may be against the vein wall).

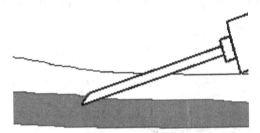

- Loosen the tourniquet. It may be obstructing blood flow.
- Try another tube. There may be no vacuum in the one being used.
- Re-anchor the vein. Veins sometimes roll away from the point of the needle and puncture site.

If Blood Stops Flowing into the Tube:

- The vein may have collapsed; resecure the tourniquet to increase venous filling. If this is not successful, remove the needle, take care of the puncture site, and redraw.

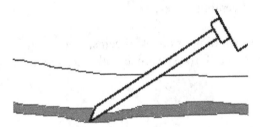

- The needle may have pulled out of the vein when switching tubes. Hold equipment firmly and place fingers against patient's arm, using the flange for leverage when withdrawing and inserting tubes.

Problems Other Than an Incomplete Collection

- A hematoma forms under the skin adjacent to the puncture site – release the tourniquet immediately and withdraw the needle. Apply firm pressure.

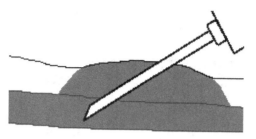

- The blood is bright red (arterial) rather than venous. Apply firm pressure for more than 5 minutes.

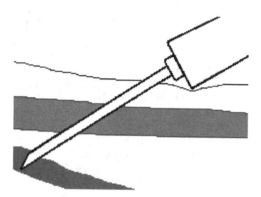

Unsuitable Veins for Venipuncture are:

- **Sclerosed veins** – these veins feel hard or cordlike. Can be caused by disease, inflammation, chemotherapy or repeated venipunctures.
- **Thrombotic veins**
- **Tortuous veins** – these are winding or crooked veins. These veins are susceptible to infection, and since blood flow is impaired, the specimen collected may produce erroneous test results.

The Phlebotomy Technician Program

Student Handout #10

VENIPUNCTURE PROCEDURE

PATIENT RELATIONS AND IDENTIFICATION

The phlebotomist's role requires a professional, courteous, and understanding manner in all contacts with the patient. Greet the patient, identify yourself and indicate the procedure that will take place. Effective communication – both verbal and nonverbal – is essential.

Proper patient identification MANDATORY. If an inpatient is able to respond, ask for a full name and always check the armband for confirmation. **DO NOT DRAW BLOOD IF THE ARMBAND IS MISSING.** An outpatient must provide identification other than the verbal statement of a name. Using the requisition for reference, ask a patient to provide additional information such as a surname or birth date.

If possible, speak with the patient during the process. The patient who is at ease will be less focused on the procedure. Always thank the patient and excuse yourself courteously when finished.

Health Care Worker Preparation

- positive attitude
- professional behavior
- preparation
- successful dialogue
- good listening skills

VENIPUNCTURE PROCEDURES

Assessing the Patient

- is the patient available?
- what age is the patient?

- what is the patient's emotional and cognitive state?
- is the patient cooperative or combative?
- are the patient's veins large or small?

Identifying the Patient

- ask the patient to state their first and last names
- compare the test requisition to the patient's ID bracelet
- for an inpatient with no ID bracelet, have a nurse place one on the patient prior to the venipuncture
- if the patient cannot have an arm bracelet, ask the nurse to ID the patient and document

Approaching the Patient

- knock on the door
- introduce yourself
- identify your position in the work place
- state your reason for being there
- wash your hands
- look for any notices above patient's bed

EQUIPMENT SELECTION

The basic step in performing venipuncture is to have the necessary supplies and/or equipment organized for proper collection of specimen and to ensure the patient's safety and comfort. The recommended supplies are as follows:

- Laboratory requisition slip and pen.
- Antiseptic –
  - Prepackaged 70% isopropyl alcohol pads are the most commonly used.
  - For collections that require more stringent infection control such as blood cultures and arterial punctures Povidone-iodine solution is commonly used.
  - For patients allergic to iodine, chlorhexidine gluconate is used.
- Vacutainer tubes –
  - Color-coded for specific tests and available in adult and pediatric sizes.
- Vacutainer needles –
  - These are disposable and are used only once both for single-tube draw and multidraw (more than one tube).
  - Needle sizes differ both in length and gauge. 1-inch and 1.5-inch long are routinely used.
  - The diameter of the bore of the needle is referred to as the gauge. The smaller the gauge the bigger the diameter of the needle; the bigger the gauge the smaller the diameter of the needle (i.e. 16 gauge is large bore and 23 gauge is small bore.) Needles smaller than 23 gauge are not used for drawing blood because they can cause hemolysis.
- Needle adapters –
  - Also called the tube holder. One end has a small opening that connects the needle, and the other end has a wide opening to hold the collection tube.
  - The needle and tube holder are called "shaft."
  - Discard the tube holder if it becomes soiled with blood.

- Winged infusion sets –
  - Used for venipuncture on small veins such as those in the hand. They are also used for venipuncture in the elderly and pediatric patients.
  - The most common size is 23 gauge, ½ to ¾ inch long.
- Sterile syringes and needles –
  - 10–20 ml syringe is used when the Vacutainer method cannot be used.
- Tourniquets –
  - Prevents the venous outflow of blood from the arm causing the veins to bulge thereby making it easier to locate the veins.
  - The most common tourniquet used is the latex strip. (Be sure to check for latex allergy). Tourniquets with Velcro and buckle closures are also available.
  - Blood pressure cuffs may also be used as tourniquet. The cuff is inflated to a pressure above the diastolic but below the systolic.
- Specimen labels –
  - To be placed on each tube collected after the venipuncture.
- Gloves –
  - Must always be worn when collecting blood specimen.
- Needle disposal container –
  - Must be a clearly marked puncture-resistant biohazard disposal container.
  - **Never recap a needle without a safety device.**

Positioning the Patient

- patients should lie or sit during venipuncture
- gently rotate the patient's arm or hand palm up to expose the antecubital area
- a pillow may be used to support the patient's arm

Venipuncture Site Selection

- look at the antecubital area of the arm
- median cubital vein
- cephalic vein
- basalic vein

CHANGES IN BLOOD CONSTITUTES THROUGHOUT THE DAY

Our bodies are constantly adapting and changing to meet its needs therefore we see changes that may occur in results based on the patient's activity, diet or what time of the day that a specimen is collected. The most common are:

- Basal State – patient is at rest in a supine position with last activity or ingestion of food being twelve hours ago
- Diurnal rhythms – are variations in our blood constitutes throughout the day
- Turbid serum – typically caused by high levels of triglycerides, cholesterol, or bacterial contamination

WHEN NOT TO USE AN ARM VEIN

Certain areas are to be avoided when choosing a site:

- Extensive scars from burns and surgery – it is difficult to puncture the scar tissue and obtain a specimen.
- The upper extremity on the side of a previous mastectomy – test results may be affected because of lymphedema.
- Hematoma – may cause erroneous test results. If another site is not available, collect the specimen distal to the hematoma.
- Intravenous therapy (IV)/blood transfusions – fluid may dilute the specimen, so collect from the opposite arm if possible. Otherwise, satisfactory samples may be drawn below the IV by following these procedures:
- Turn off the IV for at least 2 minutes before venipuncture.
- Apply the tourniquet below the IV site. Select a vein other than the one with the IV.
- Perform the venipuncture. Draw 5 ml of blood and discard before drawing the specimen tubes for testing.
- Cannula/fistula/heparin lock – hospitals have special policies regarding these devices. In general, blood should not be drawn from an arm with a fistula or cannula without consulting the attending physician.
- Edematous extremities – tissue fluid accumulation alters test results.
- Cannot draw above an IV
- Burned or scarred area
- cast or dressing on arm
- thrombosed veins
- edematous arm
- mastectomy

Tourniquet Application

- Apply at least 3 inches above the intended puncture site
- Apply firmly but not too tight that the patient is uncomfortable (applying around clothing will reduce discomfort)
- Do not place over sores or open areas
- Do not leave on for longer than one minute

Decontamination of the Puncture Site

- 70% isopropyl alcohol is most commonly used
- Gently clean area over vein
- Place all required equipment on clean surface
- Open alcohol pad and place on top of gauze
- Assemble vacutainer needle and adapter (do not remove needle cover)
- Open bandage
- Choose appropriate vacutainer tubes for ordered testing
- Apply tourniquet around patient's arm
- Ask the patient to make a fist and palpate the vein
- Put on gloves
- Place first tube in vacutainer adapter and remove needle cap
- Using other gloved hand, anchor the vein by grasping the arm just below the elbow and using only your thumb, gently pull the skin toward the wrist

- Insert the needle directly into the vein, bevel up at a 30 degree insertion level or less
- Gently push the first tube onto the needle
- As blood begins to flow, ask the patient to open their fist
- Once the tube is full remove the tube and place another tube on. Continue to do this until all required tubes are full
- If the tube has an additive, gently invert it several times when you remove it from the vacutainer
- Once all the required tubes are full, gently pull on one end of the tourniquet to remove it
- Remove the final tube and place clean gauze gently over the needle and puncture site
- Carefully remove the needle and activate the safety feature on the needle
- Apply pressure to the puncture wound until the bleeding has stopped
- Label each tube with the appropriate label
- If bleeding has stopped, apply a bandage to the wound (do not leave an infant or small child with a bandage)
- Double check the labeled tubes against the patient's armband to reconfirm identification
- Clean up patient area and dispose of sharps
- Return patient and room to the original state you found it in
- Make sure patient has their call bell
- Check side rails

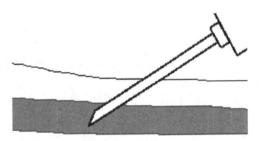

Syringe Method

- If a syringe is used, the same approach to needle insertion should take place
- Once the needle is in the vein, gently draw back on the plunger until the required amount of blood is drawn
- Do not pull too hard as this may cause hemolysis or collapse the vein
- Once you have obtained the specimen, insert the needle into the vacutainer tube. The vacutainer tube should be placed in a rack prior to performing this step
- Gently mix the additive if any and properly dispose of sharps

ORDER OF COLLECTION

The Clinical and Laboratory Standards Institute (CLSI) recommends the following specific order when collecting multiple tubes:

- Blood culture tubes (or SPS tubes)
- Blue coagulation tubes
- Gold SST or red serum tubes
- Green heparin tubes
- Lavender EDTA tubes
- Gray Fluoride tubes

Specimen Labeling

- use the labeling system provided
- place test labels on the correct tube for that specific test
- do not place more than one label on a tube
- place label with patient's name starting at the top
- place label over existing label on tube

The Phlebotomy Technician Program

Student Handout #11

CAPILLARY BLOOD SPECIMENS

SKIN PUNCTURE PROCEDURE

The distal segment of the third or fourth finger of the non-dominant hand is the recommended site. Puncture is made in the fleshy portion of the finger slightly to the side of the center perpendicular to the lines of the fingerprint.

correct

incorrect

- Wash hands
- Identify the patient
- Assemble equipment

- Warm the site: this is an essential part of the procedure when collecting specimens for pH or blood gases. Warming the site can increase the blood flow up to seven times the normal amount. The specimen is referred to as arterialized specimen because of the increase arterial flow to the area. This is accomplished by warming the site for a minimum of three minutes with a warm moistened towel (no greater than 108 F), or with a commercial warming device.
- Clean the site: Use 70% isopropyl alcohol. Allow the site to dry for maximum antiseptic action. Alcohol residue can cause hemolysis of the red blood cells and may interfere with glucose testing. Povidone – iodine (Betadine) is not used for cleaning the site because it interferes with several tests like bilirubin, uric acid, phosphorous, and potassium.
- Prepare the puncture device
- Perform the dermal puncture

Order of Draw for Capillary Specimens

- Lavender tube
- Tubes with other additives
- Tubes without additives
- Collect drops in micropipettes or microcontainers
- Apply pressure to area once you have obtained the specimen
- Assess age appropriate dressing and follow institutional guidelines
- Dispose of sharp

Labeling the Specimen

- Specimens must be labeled prior to leaving the patient's bedside
- place the label over the existing label on the tube with the name starting at the top
- for micro containers, you may flag the label around the tube or apply the label as described above and fold the extra length of label

The Phlebotomy Technician Program

Student Handout #12

SPECIMEN HANDLING, TRANSPORTATION, AND PROCESSING

SPECIMEN HANDLING AND TRANSPORTATION

Proper handling of a specimen prior to analysis is vital to the quality of the specimen. The following are the most common factors when specimen handling and transporting:

- Additive tubes should be gently mixed or inverted several times as soon as they are drawn
- Specimens must be transported gently, rough handling may hemolyze the specimen
- Non-blood specimens should be transported in leak proof containers
- Specimens should be transported in approved sealed biohazard bags

Specimens requiring protection from light should be wrapped in tin foil, they are:

- biliruben
- vitamin B12, B2, C, B6
- carotene
- red cell folate
- urine porphyrins and porphobilinogen
- erythrocyte protoporphyrin level

Specimens that need to be chilled should be transported in an ice slurry as soon as they are drawn. They are:

- blood gases
- ammonia
- lactic acid
- plasma rennin activity

- glucagons
- fibrinogen
- gastrin
- rennin

Specimens that need to be kept at 37°C are:

- cryoglobulins
- cold agglutinins – react at 4°C
- cryofibrinogen

Accepted temperatures for special transport needs are:

- body temperature – 37°C
- room Temperature – 15–30°C
- refrigerated Temperature – 2–10°C
- frozen Temperature – 220°C or lower

According to CLSI guidelines, specimens should be transported to the lab:

- the time limit for separating cells from plasma is 2 hours from collection
- specimens for glucose determinations drawn in sodium fluoride tubes are stable for 24 hours at room temperature and 48 hours refrigerated
- EDTA specimens are good for 24 hours however you must take smears with one hour of collection
- PT specimens are reliable unrefrigerated and uncentrifuged for up to 24 hours
- PTT specimens must be tested within 4 hours

Hazardous materials (laboratory specimens) transported publicly are regulated by the Department of Transport (DOT)

The Phlebotomy Technician Program

Student Handout #13

PEDIATRIC AND GERIATRIC PROCEDURES

PEDIATRIC PROCEDURES

The heel is used for dermal punctures on infants less than 1 year of age. Areas recommended are the medial and lateral areas of the plantar surface of the foot. These are determined by drawing imaginary lines medially extending from the middle of the great toe to the heel and laterally from the middle of the fourth and fifth toes to the heel.

The American Academy of Pediatrics recommends that heel punctures for infants not exceed 2.0 mm.

Observe the following precautions when performing dermal puncture:

- do not puncture deeper than 2.0 mm
- do not perform dermal punctures on previous puncture sites
- do not use the back of the heel or arch of the foot
- use the lateral posterior area of the plantar surface of the heel

Preparing the Child:

- introduce yourself
- correctly identify patient
- ask about previous venipuncture experience
- develop a plan with the parent

- be honest
- encourage parent involvement
- explain the procedure
- establish guidelines

OTHER CONSIDERATIONS

Age specific considerations are

- equipment preparation
- positioning or restraining the child
- combative patients
- interventions to alleviate pain

- pacifier
- emotions of the parent
- use treatment room rather than patient room if available

Total Blood Volumes

- premature infant: 115 mL/kg
- newborn: 80–110 mL/kg
- infant and children: 75–100 mL/kg
- example: 3kg (6.6 lbs) infant would have a total blood volume of 225 to 300 mL

BLOOD COLLECTION ON BABIES

The recommended location for blood collection on a newborn baby or infant is the heel. The diagram indicates the darkened area as the proper area to use for heel punctures for blood collection:

Prewarming the infant's heel (39 to 42° C for 3 to 5 minutes) is important to obtain capillary blood/blood gas samples and warming also greatly increases the flow of blood for collection of other specimens and can increase blood flow up to 7 times. However, do not use too high a temperature warmer, because baby's skin is thin and susceptible to thermal injury.

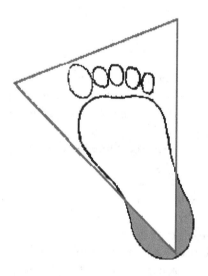

Equipment for Micro Sample

- pediatric safety lancet device
- alcohol swab
- gauze
- capillary tubes and sealer
- capillary collection tubes

- sharps container
- gloves
- bandage
- labels or requisition

Micro Procedure

- wash hands
- put on gown
- obtain equipment
- identify patient
- apply gloves
- warm heel
- perform heel puncture
- wipe away first drop of blood
- gently milk heel to obtain specimens
- hold gauze over site until bleeding stops
- place bandage over site
- label all tubes
- remove all collection supplies from crib
- make sure baby is OK

Precautions

- a baby's heel may be punctured a maximum of two times
- do not puncture an area that is bruised or sloughing skin is present
- warm the heel
- use only gentle massaging when milking the heel
- never re-puncture old puncture sites
- never pick up the baby
- the maximum length for a lancet used to puncture a baby's heel is 2.4 mm
- capillary blood gases requires that the site be warmed prior to puncture
- a potential for complications when accidentally puncturing the calcaneus bone is osteochondritis and osteomyelitis as well as possible sepsis if an organism is introduced
- red cell counts are higher in newborns than adults
- excessive squeezing may cause an elevated biliruben

NEONATAL SCREENING

PKU Procedure:

- perform puncture
- the collection card will have circles at one end of the card
- place the back of the first circle against the puncture site. Continue to mild puncture site until the circle is filled in
- repeat until all circles are filled in
- filter paper specimens should be dried at 20°C horizontally for at least 4 hours
- specimens should be mailed for analysis within 24 hours
- used to screen for congenital hypothyroidism

Unsatisfactory PKU Testing

- all circles not filled
- circles over filled
- card placed in envelope to be mailed to the state before specimen is dry
- form completed improperly
- specimen not sent to lab within 24 hours

DORSAL HAND VENIPUNCTURE

- dorsal hand procedure
- ID patient

- place a tourniquet just above the wrist
- gently grasping the fingers in a fist tilt the wrist downward
- gently palpate the veins in the back of the hand
- using a butterfly, insert the needle at a 15 degree angle

Considerations for the Elderly

- hearing loss
- failing eyesight
- loss of taste, smell and feeling
- memory loss
- epithelium and subcutaneous tissue becomes thinner
- muscles become smaller
- increase susceptibility to hypothermia
- emotional problems

The Phlebotomy Technician Program

Student Handout #14

POINT OF CARE COLLECTIONS

I. Demand for point-of-care testing (POCT) is increasing because rapid turnaround of laboratory test results is necessary.

   1. POCT instruments use small amounts of uncentrifuged blood specimens

   2. Use of skin puncture blood, urine, or saliva

   3. Frequently Used Point-of-Care Tests
      a. Glucose
      b. Electrolytes and Blood Gas Analytes
      c. Hemoglobin A1c
      d. Hemoglobin
      e. Infectious diseases (i.e., HIV)
      f. Influenza A and B
      g. Lipids (Cholesterol, HDL Cholesterol, LDL Cholesterol)
      h. Pregnancy
      i. Triglycerides
      j. Brain natriuretic peptide (BNP)

II. Glucose Monitoring

A. Diabetes Mellitus

1. A chronic disease in which the pancreas cannot produce enough insulin or cannot use the insulin that it does produce.
2. Insulin causes the glucose to be absorbed from the blood into the body tissues and then used for energy.
3. The lack of insulin in patients with diabetes mellitus leads to increased blood glucose levels.

B. Glucose Meters

- Skin puncture from the finger.
- Heel stick (for infants).
- Flushed heparin line.
- Safety and quality control protocols must be followed.
- HemoCue Glucose Analyzer.
- Nova StatStrip.

C. Obtaining Blood Specimen for Glucose Testing (Skin Puncture)

- Select the site and cleanse it with antiseptic (especially the side of a finger).
- Cleanse the skin with an alcohol wipe and allow the skin to dry.
- Gently massage the finger a few times from base to tip to aid blood flow.
- Decide on which side of the finger to make the incision.
- Remove the safety lancet from the protective paper without touching the tip and, as you hold the patient's finger firmly with one hand, make a swift, deep puncture with the retractable safety puncture device.
- Wipe the first three drops of blood away with clean gauze.
- Gently massage the finger from base to tip to obtain the needed drop of blood. Do not squeeze the fingertip because this can cause hemolysis of the blood sample.
- Apply the HemoCue® microcuvette to the drop of blood. The correct volume is drawn into the cuvette by capillary action (capillary, venous, or arterial blood can be used).
- Wipe off any excess blood from the sides of the cuvette.
- Place the microcuvette into the cuvette holder and insert it into the photometer.
- The laboratory test result is displayed automatically.
- Discard the safety automatic lancet in the sharps container with biohazard label.

III. Quality in Point-of-Care Testing and Disinfecting Analyzers

- Calibrated with Standards (calibrators)
- Monitored with Quality Control Material
- Electronic Quality Control (EQC)
- Mean (average), Standard Deviation (SD), and QC Charts
- Reproducibility of the Results: Purchasing the reagent strips and controls in quantities that enable health care workers to use constant pools of the same lot number
- Preventive Maintenance: Required preventive maintenance of each point-of-care instrument is critical for accurate results
- Problems to Avoid in Point-of-Care Testing
- Routine cleaning of the POCT instruments is needed to avoid transmission of nosocomial infections

IV. Blood Gas and Electrolyte Analysis

- Measurement of the pO_2, pCO_2, and pH
  - The pO_2 and pCO_2 are analyzed whenever a patient has a heart or lung disorder.
  - The blood pH determines whether the blood is too acidic or too alkaline.
  - Measurement of Blood Electrolyte Levels—Na^+, K^+, Cl^-, Ca^{++}.
- Point-of-Care Testing for Acute Heart Damage
  - Measurement of Troponin T
  - Assay uses whole venous blood
  - ROCHE TROPT Sensitive Rapid Assay
- Blood Coagulation Monitoring
  - Immediate Results Used in Controlling Bleeding or Clotting Disorders in Patients
  - CoaguChek S System
  - The ITC, Inc. ProTime (PT/INR)
- Monitor Long-Term Anticoagulation Therapy in Patients
  - Actalyke Activated Clotting Time Test (ACT) System
  - The Hemochron Jr. Instrument
  - The Rapidpoint Coag Analyzer
  - The INRatio Meter
- Hematocrit, Hemoglobin, and other Hematology Parameters
  - Hematocrit (Hct, packed cell volume [PCV], Crit)
    - Represents the volume of circulating blood that is occupied by red blood cells (RBCs).
    - It is expressed as a percentage.
    - Values are obtained to aid in the diagnosis and evaluation of anemia.
    - Blood collection usually occurs by skin puncture.
    - Plastic microcapillary tubes are used.
- Hemoglobin
  - More accurate than hematocrit.
  - Safer method to detect anemia.
  - HemoCue-Hemoglobin System.
  - The Ichor automated cell counter.

V. Cholesterol Screening

- Using a finger stick drop of blood, total cholesterol (TC) values can be obtained.
  - Cholestech LDX System
  - TC
  - HDL cholesterol
  - LDL cholesterol

VI. Bleeding-Time Test

- Useful Tool for Testing Platelet Plug Formation
- Performed by Minor Standardized Incision on the Forearm
- Recording the Length of Time Required for Bleeding to Cease
- Surgicutt Bleeding-Time Test
  - Prior to procedure, patients should be advised of scarring.
  - Materials and supplies should be prepared before beginning the procedure.
    - Surgicutt instrument
    - Gloves
    - Antiseptic swab

- Blood pressure cuff (sphygmomanometer)
- Surgicutt bleeding-time blotting paper disk
- Butterfly-type bandage
- Place the patient's arm on a steady support with the volar surface exposed. The incision is best performed over the lateral aspect.
- Incision over volar surface of the forearm.
- Inflate the BP cuff to 40 mm Hg for adults.
- Cleanse the area and remove the Surgicutt device from package.
- Remove the safety clip.
- Hold the device securely between the thumb and the middle finger.
- Gently push the trigger, starting the stopwatch, and remove the device from the patient's forearm immediately after triggering.
- Wick the blood every 30 seconds.
- Remove BP cuff, cleanse the incision site, and apply the nonallergenic butterfly-type bandage.
- Possible Interfering Factors.

The ingestion of aspirin-containing products up to 7 to 10 days prior to testing may affect results. Other drugs (e.g., dextran, streptokinase, streptodornase, ethyl alcohol, mithramycin) may cause a prolonged bleeding time.

In the past, the primary screen for platelet dysfunction was the bleeding time. However, the bleeding time procedure has fallen from favor in recent years. Many hospitals are no longer offering it, and several national organizations have issued position statements against its routine use as a pre-surgical screen. The bleeding time is not sensitive or specific, and it does not necessarily reflect the risk or severity of surgical bleeding. It is poorly reproducible, can be affected by aspirin ingestion and by the skill of the person performing the test, and frequently leaves small thin scars on the forearm.

The PFA (Platelet Function Analysis) is a testing device that many hospitals are using as a platelet function screen, in place of the bleeding time, to mimic the clotting process. The phlebotomist draws one or two (depending on the lab's policy) cc of blood in a light blue top tube (Buffered Na Citrate 3.2%) from a vein in the arm. This is NOT a POCT test. It must be performed in the lab. Other considerations for the phlebotomist when obtaining a specimen for a PFA test are:

- The tube must be filled with a ratio of 9:1 blood to additive
- Mix thoroughly by gentle inversion
- Deliver immediately to the laboratory at room temperature
- Do not put through the pneumatic tube
- **Do Not** draw through a heparinized line
- **Do Not** Refrigerate
- **Do Not** centrifuge

VII. Other POCT Tests and Future Trends

- Hemoglobin A1c Procedure
- Noninvasively Measure Concentration of Bilirubin
- Rapid HIV Point-of-Care Test
- Point-of-Learning for New POCT

The Phlebotomy Technician Program

Student Handout #15

ARTERIAL, INTRAVENOUS (IV), AND SPECIAL COLLECTION PROCEDURES

ARTERIAL BLOOD GASES

This test is performed to perform blood analysis for arterial blood gases.

MODIFIED ALLEN PROCEDURE

This procedure is performed to check for collateral circulation to the hand prior to performing an arterial stick on the radial artery:

- Have patient make a tight fist
- Using the middle and index fingers of both hands compress the radial and ulnar arteries located on both sides of the patient's inner wrist
- While maintaining pressure, have the patient open their hand, the hand should be blanched or drained of color
- Lower the patient's hand and release pressure on the ulnar artery only while keeping pressure on the radial artery
- For a positive Allen's test, the hand should begin to pinken-up within 15 seconds. If the test is positive, you can procedure with the arterial puncture

- If the hand does not pinken-up in this time period, you have a negative Allen's test and another site must be chosen for the arterial puncture

To perform this test, do the following:

- locate the radial artery at the inside of the wrist
- you will feel the pulse of the artery
- clean area with iodine
- use all universal precautions
- no tourniquet is used
- a prefilled heparin safety syringe is used
- spread skin with finger taunt
- pierce the pulsating artery at 30–45 degree angle
- the blood will flow into the syringe on its own
- withdraw fill syringe and place firm pressure on puncture site for at least 5 minutes
- cover syringe and place syringe in an airtight container of icy water to decrease the loss of gas during transportation
- check for bleeding and apply pressure bandage
- other sites that can be used are the brachial artery: located in the cubital fossa of the arm and the femoral artery: located in the groin area of the leg

LINE DRAWS

There are several types of line draws listed below. It is important to remember that lines commonly contain an anticoagulant such as heparin. Therefore the first 10 mL of blood drawn from a line must be waste. Most facilities require that line draws be performed by the nurse.

- central intravenous line (CVC) (VAD) – inserted in the subclavian vein, superior vena cava or jugular vein
- peripherally inserted central catheter (PICC) – inserted in the basilic or cephalic vein – should not be used, as can collapse during blood draw
- heparin lock – inserted into VAD for blood draws or medication

SPECIAL VENIPUNCTURE

Some venipunctures are done using special collecting or handling procedures specific to the test being requested. Some require patient preparation such as fasting, while some need to be collected at a specific time. Still others may need special handling such as protection from light.

FASTING SPECIMENS

This requires collection of blood while the patient is in the basal state, that is, the patient has fasted and refrained from strenuous exercise for 12 hours prior to the drawing. It is the phlebotomist's responsibility to verify if the patient indeed, has been fasting for the required time.

HEMOGLOBIN A1C

A blood test (also known as glycated hemoglobin) that provides the physician with a picture of a patient's average blood glucose control for the past 2 to 3 months.

BLOOD BANK SPECIMENS

Blood bank specimens require a plain red top tube or a pink or lavender top EDTA tube. Strict procedures must be followed when identifying the patient and labeling the specimen.

LABELING THE SPECIMEN

Blood bank specimens require the following information:

- Patient's full name including middle initial
- Hospital ID #
- Date of birth
- Date and time of collection
- Phlebotomist's initials
- Room # and Bed #

TYPE AND CROSS MATCH

This test screens donated blood for compatibility with a possible patient transfusion. It is vital that all procedures be followed. Each facility will have a system in place that must be strictly followed. This procedure generally requires that a special band be filled out and placed on the patient's arm. Each band is labeled with identification numbers and these numbers are also placed on the specimens that are collected at that time for the transfusion procedure.

Donor Room Collections

- a 17 g thin walled needle is used
- the patient must have a minimum hematocrit value of 38% to be a blood donor
- blood is usually obtained from the antecubital area of the arm
- patient is placed in semi-prone position
- patient should never be left alone while collecting donor blood
- as the collection begins, the needle and tubing should be taped to the patient's arm
- the donor should be encouraged to continue to slowly open and close the hand during donation
- the blood in the bag must be mixed with the anticoagulant during collection
- once 405 to 495 mL is collected the tubing is clamped off, the tourniquet released, the needle removed and pressure applied to the site
- PCV – packed cell volume

BLOOD CULTURES

They are ordered to detect presence of microorganisms in the patient's blood. The patient will usually have chills and fever of unknown origin (FUO), indicating the possible presence of pathogenic micro-organisms in the blood (septicemia). Blood cultures are usually ordered STAT or as timed specimen, and collection requires strict aseptic technique.

Supplies

- gloves and tourniquet
- three alcohol preps
- blood culture prep kit
- two blood culture vials (anaerobic and aerobic)
- needle 23 gauge or butterfly
- syringe
- gauze
- bandage

Procedure

- clean intended venipuncture site and tops of culture bottles with alcohol pads
- open blood culture prep kit and remove frepp
- hold in horizontal position and pinch the handle to break ampule.
- place frepp on venipuncture site and scrub for 60 seconds
- remove the sepp (iodine ampule), hold in downward position and pinch center to crush ampule
- apply iodine to the venipuncture site starting at the center and moving outwards in concentric circles to the periphery (about 2 inches)
- allow to stand about 30 to 60 seconds to dry
- perform the venipuncture and collect a minimum of 3 cc for each bottle for an adult and 1 cc for a child
- a new venipuncture must be performed for each set of blood cultures

It is vital that contamination of the site or equipment does not occur

POSTPRANDIAL GLUCOSE TEST

Postprandial means after meals. This test is used to evaluate diabetes mellitus. Fasting glucose level is compared with the level 2 hours after eating a full meal or ingesting a measured amount of glucose.

Procedure

- the patient arrives at the lab fasting
- a fasting specimen is obtained
- the patient leaves and eats a high carbohydrate, high glucose meal
- patient returns to have their blood drawn 2 hours after they have finished eating

GLUCOSE TOLERANCE TEST – PATIENT SHOULD REFRAIN FROM STRENUOUS EXERCISE 12 HOURS PRIOR TO THE TEST

This test is used to diagnose diabetes mellitus and evaluate patients with frequent low blood sugar. 3-hour OGTT is used to test hyperglycemia (abnormally high blood sugar level) and diagnose diabetes mellitus. 5-hour OGTT is used to evaluate hypoglycemia (abnormally low blood sugar level) for disorders of carbohydrate metabolism. OGTT are scheduled to begin between 0700 and 0900.

Supplies

- venipuncture supplies
- glucose
- requisition or labels
- urine collection supplies

Procedure

- patient must be fasting
- explain procedure to the patient
- may be ordered as 2, 3, 4 or 5 hour test
- perform venipuncture and collect a fasting specimen
- have patient give a fasting urine specimen
- administer glucose:
  - non pregnant persons – 75 gm
  - pregnant – 100 gm
  - child – based on weight, 1.75 gm per kg weight to a maximum of 75 gm
- the dose of glucose must be consumed within 5 minutes
- the test begins when the patient has finished the drink
- the time is noted and all subsequent samples are based on this time
- blood and urine specimens are then collected 30 minutes and 1, 2, 3 and four hours from the time the drink was finished
- the patient cannot eat or drink anything but water during the test
- the patient cannot smoke
- if the patient vomits during the test, the test is canceled
- the patient must be monitored for any signs of problems, sweating, nausea, drowsiness, confusion
- in an outpatient setting, some hospitals require that the fasting specimen be tested on site using a glucometer
- if the fasting specimen results are 150 or higher, the patient's physician is to be called and an order obtained to discontinue or proceed with the test

THERAPEUTIC DRUG MONITORING (TDM)

This test is used to evaluate the following:

- a highly toxic drug
- underdosing or overdosing
- alterations in drugs due to multiple medications
- aminoglycosides are TDM drugs
- rate the med. is metabolized
- effectiveness of drug

TROUGH AND PEAK

This test is used to monitor the blood levels of certain medication to ensure patient safety and also maintain a plasma level. Blood is drawn to coincide with the trough (lowest blood level) or the peak level (highest blood level). Trough levels are collected immediately before the scheduled dose. Time for collecting peak level will vary depending on the medication, patient's metabolism, and the route of administration (I.V., I.M., or oral).

- TROUGH: called trough because the blood is drawn at the time of drug's lowest concentration in the system

- PEAK: called peak because the specimen represents the highest concentration of med in patient's system

Timed Specimens

They are often used to monitor the level of a specific substance or condition in the patient. Blood is drawn at specific times for different reasons. They are:

- To measure blood levels of substances exhibiting diurnal variation. (e.g., cortisol hormone)
- To determine blood levels of medications. (e.g., digoxin for cardiovascular disease)
- To monitor changes in a patient's condition. (e.g., steady decrease in hemoglobin)

The most common reasons to have a specimen drawn at a specific time are:

- monitor OD
- determine dosage of med
- establish baseline following medication for new drug therapy
- within 6 hours of a seizure
- drug toxicity is suspected
- check medication level

STAT, ASAP, Timed

- STATS: must be collected within 20 minutes of the time the order was received
- NOW/ASAP: must be collected with one hour of the time the order was received
- TIMED: must be collected at a specific time

BLEEDING TIME TEST

This test is performed to monitor platelet function and blood vessel integrity. There are two types of bleeding time tests. The first one is Duke's bleeding time which is rarely ordered today. It is performed on the earlobe. The more common procedure is called the Ivy bleeding time and requires the following:

Supplies

- surgicutt instrument
- gloves
- antiseptic swab
- blood pressure cuff
- filter paper disk
- butterfly bandage
- stop watch

Procedure

- patient should be informed that test may cause small scarring
- place patient's arm on steady support
- choose a puncture site away from any visible veins on the forearm on the lateral aspect, volar surface of the forearm
- place the BP cuff on patient's arm above the antecubital crease and inflate to 40 mm Hg
- apply gloves and cleanse area (cleaning of the area too vigorously may result in hyperemia)

- place surgicutt device against arm parallel to the antecubital crease and activate device (the cut must be made no longer than 60 seconds after the BP cuff has been inflated)
- start stop watch
- use filter paper to soak up blood about every thirty seconds until bleeding stops
- do not touch the site with the filter paper
- once bleeding stops, stop the watch and remove blood pressure cuff
- apply butterfly bandage over site bringing edges of cut together
- instruct patient to leave on for 24 hours
- document time result
- patient use of aspirin and salicylic acid can interfere with the BT results from 7 to 10 days

COLD AGGLUTININS

Cold agglutinins are antibodies produced in response to Mycoplasma pneumoniae infection (atypical pneumonia). The antibodies formed may attach to red blood cells at temperatures below body temperature, and as such, the specimen must be kept warm until the serum is separated from the cells. Blood is collected in red-topped tubes pre-warmed in the incubator at 37 degrees Celsius for 30 minutes.

CHILLED SPECIMENS

Some tests require that the specimen collected be chilled immediately after collection in crushed ice or ice and water mixture. Likewise, the specimen must be immediately transported to the laboratory for processing. Some of the tests that require chilled specimen are: arterial blood gases, ammonia, lactic acid, pyruvate, ACTH, gastrin, and parathyroid hormone.

PROTECTION FROM LIGHT

Specimens are protected from light by wrapping the tubes in aluminum foil immediately after they are drawn. Exposure to light could alter the test results for: Bilirubin, beta-carotene, Vitamins A & B6, and porphyrins.

The Phlebotomy Technician Program

Student Handout #16

URINALYSIS, BODY FLUIDS, AND OTHER SPECIMENS

CLEAN CATCH URINE

Supplies

- Sterile container
- Antiseptic towelettes

Procedure: Women

- after washing hands, the women should separate the skin folds around the urinary opening
- using the towelettes, clean the area, wiping from back to front
- holding the skin folds apart, urinate the first part of the flow into the toilet, the middle stream into the container, and the remainder into the toilet
- the container must not touch the genital area
- the inside of the lid must not touch any surface

Procedure: Men

- the man should wash his hands
- using the towelettes, wash the end of the penis, if the man is not circumcised, the fore skin is to be retracted and the area cleansed with the towelettes

- the initial urine is to be placed in the toilet, the middle of the stream is to be collected in the container, being careful not to make skin contact with the container
- the inside of the lid is not to make contact with any surface

24 HOUR URINE COLLECTION

Supplies

- 3–4 L container with tight fitting lid
- preservative/additive if required
- label for bottle

Procedure

- label the container including the patient name, date of collection, ID #, start and end time of collection
- test is to be started the following morning with the first specimen being discarded into the toilet
- from that point on, all urine is to be collected in the container for a period of 24 hours
- the first urine of the following morning is to be collected in the container
- the container of urine is to be kept in a cool environment

OTHER BODY FLUIDS

Seminal Fluid

- collected in clean container and delivered to the lab within 2 hours

Synovial Fluid

- Fluid collected from a joint by a physician with a sterile syringe and placed in a sterile container

Amniotic Fluid

- Collected by a physician, must be protected from light

Sputum

- Collected in clean container

FECAL SPECIMENS

Stool specimens are commonly tested for:

- O&P
- Occult blood
- enteric organisms (salmonella)
- virus

Ova and Parasites

- specimen collected in a large mouth plastic container
- patient instructed not to urinate in the specimen
- maintain at body temperature
- properly labeled and returned to the lab
- with an infant, the specimen can be collected in a diaper

Occult Blood

- Requires 3 special tests cards
- the stool is collected in a clean container
- a small smear of stool is placed on the testing area of the card and the cover closed on the card
- requested information on the front of the card is filled out by the patient
- the procedure is repeated on two additional cards

SWEAT CHLORIDE TEST

A sweat chloride test is performed on all infants with a positive newborn screen and any individual with symptoms and tests for cystic fibrosis. A sweat sample is collected using a special sweat stimulation procedure. A tiny amount of a sweat-stimulating liquid is applied to a small patch of skin on the arm or leg. An electrode is then placed over the site and a weak electrical current stimulates the area. After several minutes, the area is cleaned and sweat is collected for about thirty minutes, either into a plastic coil of tubing or onto a piece of gauze or filter paper. The sweat obtained is then analyzed.

The Phlebotomy Technician Program

Student Handout #17

DRUG USE, FORENSIC TOXICOLOGY, WORKPLACE TESTING, SPORTS MEDICINE, AND RELATED AREAS

I. Overview and Prevalence of Drug Use

- Illicit Drugs
  - Marijuana
  - Cocaine
  - Heroin
  - Hallucinogens
  - Inhalants
  - Nonmedical use of prescription-type drugs
  - Gateway Drugs
    - Alcohol
    - Tobacco
- Facts about Substance Abuse
  - Most addictions develop during adolescence.
  - Illicit drug users by age category in the U.S.:
    - Ages 12–17, 2.4 million people
    - Ages 18–25, 6.5 million
    - Ages 26 and over, 11 million

- Among adolescents 12–17 years, drugs used vary by age (common ones are prescription-type drugs used for nonmedical uses, marijuana, inhalants, followed by hallucinogens and cocaine).

II. Common Drug Analysis Methods and Interferences

- Immunoassays
- Useful for qualitative screening, rapid turn around, and low cost.
  - Thin Layer Chromatography
  - Quantitative method but uses older technology, requires additional skills to run the analysis.
  - Can be used to test for multiple drugs at one time.
- Gas Chromatography – Mass Spectrometry
  - Quantitative method with highest degree of specificity for drug detection, often used to confirm screening results; however, it is more expensive and time consuming.
  - Interfering substances (poppy seeds, teas, ibuprofen, salicylates, dextromethorphan, fluconazole, narcotic analgesics)

III. Forensic Toxicology Specimens

- Definitions: Toxicology, Forensic Specimens
  - Toxicology is the scientific study of poisons (including drugs), how they are detected, their actions in the human body, and the treatment of the conditions they produce.
  - Forensic specimens are those involved in civil or criminal legal cases. They may be decomposing or exposed to elements, available only in trace amounts, and/or collected postmortem.
- Examples of Forensic Specimens
  - Anorectal swabs
  - Arterial blood
  - Bones
  - Capillary blood
  - Clothing
  - Dried blood stains
  - Hair
  - Nails, nail scrapings, or clippings
  - Saliva
  - Skin
  - Sperm, semen residue
  - Sweat
  - Teeth, oral swabs
  - Urine
  - Venous blood
  - Vaginal swabs
- Crime Laboratories
  - Analyze trace evidence (fingerprints, hair or fibers, fragments of evidence, firearms and toolmarks, drug chemistry, toxicology, arson and fire debris, body stains, documents, and computers)
- DNA in Forensic Applications
  - Useful because of its accuracy. It is the same in all cells of the body (except eggs and sperm cells, which contain one-half of the DNA).
  - It stays the same throughout life.
  - It is present in all cells.
  - It differs from one person to another, except in the case of identical twins.

IV. Chain of Custody

- Definitions: Chain of Custody, Tamper-Evident Seal
  - Chain of custody is the process for maintaining control and accountability of each specimen from the time it is collected to time of disposal.
  - The process documents the identity of each individual that handles the specimen and each time a specimen is transferred in the chain.
  - A chain of custody form is also required that indicates specific identification of the patient or subject, the individual who obtained and processed the specimen, the date, the location, and the signature of the subject documenting that the specimen in the container is the one that was obtained from the person identified on the label.
  - The specimen must be placed in a specimen transfer bag that is permanently sealed until it is opened for analysis.

V. Workplace Drug Testing

- Drug Testing in the Workplace
  - Workplace drug testing programs are used for one or more of the following reasons:
  - To comply with federal regulations (DOT, DOD, NRC, DOE)
  - To comply with customer or contract requirements and insurance carrier requirements
  - To minimize the chances of hiring employees who are drug users/abusers
  - To reinforce the policy of "no drug use"
  - To identify users and refer them for assistance
  - To establish reasons for disciplinary actions
  - To improve safety and health of employees, reduce addiction
- Type of industries where antidrug programs are required (aviation, highway, railroad, mass transit, pipeline, hazmat transport, maritime, etc.)
- Situations where drug testing is appropriate or necessary include
  - Pre-employment testing: Job offers are made after a negative drug test.
  - Pre-promotion tests: Testing employees prior to making a promotion.
  - Annual physical tests: To identify users/abusers so they can be referred for assistance and/or disciplinary action.
  - Reasonable suspicion/for-cause tests: For employees who show signs of being impaired or have documented patterns of unsafe work practices.
  - Random tests: Commonly used in safety or security-sensitive jobs, involves testing at unpredictable times.
  - Post-accident tests: Used to determine if drugs or alcohol were a factor in an employee who was involved in an incident and/or accident.
  - Treatment follow-up or clearance to return to work: Periodic testing for employees after participating in a rehabilitation program.
  - Return to work clearance (after a rehab program).
  - Compliance with child- or elder-abuse investigations.
  - Operation of company vehicles if behavior is suspect.
- The consequences of testing positive involve the following:
  - Employers with workplace testing programs have guidelines in place that should explain procedures for what actions are taken after a positive test (paid or unpaid leave, referral to an employee assistance program, automatic discharge, disciplinary actions, and/or appeals procedures).
- Testing procedures.
  - Institutional procedures for drug testing are normally a part of the workplace drug-testing program.

- Information may include where samples will be collected and tested, how results will be reported, the chain of custody, the drugs and cutoff levels used to determine if a test is positive or negative, and the confirmatory tests used if the initial test is positive.
- The time to detect drugs is dependent on metabolic rate, dose of the drug, how it was taken, and the cutoff concentrations used by each laboratory. Generally drugs are detectable for several days.
- Employees should be aware of the procedures.

VI. Tampering with Specimens

- Adulteration
  - Adulteration is a means of tampering with the specimen, usually urine, to make the specimen test negatively for drugs.
  - It occurs in two ways:
    - When substances are ingested by the patient to alter his/her own urine.
    - When substances are added or substituted for urine at the time of collection.
    - Water is the most common substance added to the specimen or ingested to dilute the urine.
    - Liquid soap, bleach, salt, ammonia, vinegar, baking soda, UrinAid (glutaraldehyde), Klear (potassium nitrite), lemon juice, cologne.
- Detecting Adulterants
  - Sensory examination
  - Urine temperature
  - Simple tests for detection
  - Adding bluing to the toilet water
  - Direct observation of devices (tubing attached to the person)

VII. Drug Use in Sports

- NCAA, NBA, NFL, Olympics
- Drug-Use and Performance Enhancing Substances
  - Nutritional supplements (not regulated by FDA) may lead to positive tests.
  - Stimulants.
  - Anabolic steroids, hormones.
  - Street drugs, etc.
- Blood Doping and Use of Erythropoietin
  - Whole blood, packed red blood cells, or blood substitutes (EPO or recombinant human erythropoietin) are injected intravenously in athletes who try to increase their endurance.
  - Increases the body's oxygen-carrying capacity.
  - Detected in the laboratory using hematology parameters and isoelectric focusing techniques.

VIII. Preferred Specimens for Drug Tests

- Blood: Best specimen for alcohol and EPO testing
- Urine
  - Preferred specimen in sports drug testing.
  - Drugs and their metabolites are present in higher concentrations in urine than in blood.
  - Large specimen volumes are easily obtainable.
  - There is no pain or discomfort to the athlete when collecting the specimen.
  - The process of collection is noninvasive.
  - Disadvantages are the risks of tampering and short detection times from the drug use.

- Hair
  - Detection times for drugs in human hair range from weeks to months.
  - It is costly.
  - Infrequent drug use will not likely be detected.
- Neonatal Drug Testing
  - Determined by using the maternal history, newborn clinical symptoms, and laboratory toxicology testing of the mother and infant.
  - Cocaine is the drug most often identified in neonatal drug testing.
  - Urine is the specimen most often used for neonatal drug exposure.
  - Meconium is also used for drug analysis. It is the first intestinal discharge of a neonate, is greenish, and consists of epithelial cells, mucus, and bile.

IX. Blood Alcohol and Breath Testing

- Drunk driving is illegal in all 50 states.
  - Most countries (including U.S.) have legal limits for blood alcohol concentration/content (BAC), expressed as a percentage. In U.S. BAC is 0.08%, or 80 mg per 100 mL in most states.
- Many analyzers and methods for testing alcohol levels in blood, breath, and urine. Obtaining blood specimens from patients varies in each state. Blood specimens are the most accurate.
- If blood alcohol specimens are collected by venipuncture or finger punctures, all procedures are similar to routine collections, except that the phlebotomist must use a nonalcoholic disinfectant to cleanse the site.
- Patient variables that affect the BAC are sex, weight, amount of alcohol ingested, other foods ingested, time elapsed since ingestion, and other drugs ingested.
- Breathalyzers commonly used by law enforcement personnel due to ease of use, less invasive, and portability. However, there is wide variability in accuracy of measurement.
- Advantages of Breath Testing
  - The procedure does not require trained laboratory staff.
  - The sample collection is noninvasive.
  - The analysis is fast.
  - Results are quickly available and easy to read.
  - The procedure is less costly.

PART C
Phlebotomy Technician

STUDENT GRADUATE
ASSISTANCE PACKET

TABLE OF CONTENTS

Note: This packet can be used by students interested in finding employment in health care as well as other related fields. The information in this packet includes helpful hints, best practices, interview techniques and other information to assist students in their search for life long employment.

The Phlebotomy Technician Program

INTRODUCTION

Your hands are damp as you wring them uncontrollably. Your mouth is dry, and you wonder if the right words will ever escape you lips. Your stomach is doing loop-de-loops as you make yet another run for the bathroom. And this is only the day before the interview!

Does this sound like you? You're not alone. It is very common, and normal, to be nervous before an interview. Feeling anxious will raise your energy level, and that's a good thing, just be sure you don't get too nervous. The best way to avoid common job search and interview mistakes is to prepare.

The Phlebotomy Technician Program

THE RESUME

Your resume is a tool with one specific purpose: to win an interview. A resume is an advertisement, nothing more, nothing less.

A great resume doesn't just tell them what you have done but makes the same assertion that all good ads do: If you buy this product (Me), you will get these specific, direct benefits. It presents you in the best light. It convinces the employer that you have what it takes to be successful in this new position or career.

It is so pleasing to the eye that the reader is enticed to pick it up and read it. It "whets the appetite," stimulates interest in meeting you and learning more about you. It inspires the prospective employer to pick up the phone and ask you to come in for an interview.

Your cover letter should make the reader want to learn more about you and provide a preview to your resume. It should not provide the same details as your resume but act as an introduction to your resume.

When creating your resume, use the following guidelines:

- **The resume is visually enticing**, a work of art. Simple clean structure. Very easy to read . . . Uncrowded.
- **There is uniformity and consistency in the use of italics, capital letters, bullets, boldface, and underlining.** For example, if a period is at the end of one job's dates, a period should be at the end of all jobs' dates.
- **There are absolutely no errors.** No typographical errors. No spelling errors. No grammar, syntax, or punctuation errors. No errors of fact.
- **All the basic, expected information is included.** A resume must have the following key information: your name, address, phone number, and your email address at the top of the first page, a listing of jobs held, in reverse chronological order, educational degrees including the highest degree received, in reverse chronological order. Additional, targeted information will of course accompany this.

- **Jobs listed** include a title, the name of the firm, the city and state of the firm, and the years.
- **It is targeted.** A resume should be targeted to your goal, to the ideal next step in your career.
- **Strengths are highlighted/weaknesses de-emphasized.** Focus on whatever is strongest and most impressive.
- **Use power words.** For every skill, accomplishment, or job described, use the most active impressive verb you can think of (which is also accurate).
- **Show you are results-oriented.** Wherever possible, prove that you have the desired qualifications through a clear strong statement of accomplishments . . . For example: "Initiated and directed complete automation of the Personnel Department, resulting in time-cost savings of over 25%."
- **Writing is concise and to the point.** Keep sentences as short and direct as possible.
- **Make it look great.** Use a laser printer or an ink jet printer that produces high-quality results. Use a standard conservative typeface (font) in 11 or 12 point. Don't make them squint to read it. Use off-white, ivory or bright white 8 1/2 × 11-inch paper, in the highest quality affordable.
- **Shorter is usually better.** Everyone freely gives advice on resume length. Most of these self-declared experts say a resume should always be one page.
- **Break it up.** A good rule is to have no more than six lines of writing in any one writing "block" or paragraph (summary, skill section, accomplishment statement, job description, etc.). If any more than this is necessary, start a new section or a new paragraph.
- **Experience before education . . . usually.** Experience sections should come first, before education, in most every case.
- **Telephone number that will be answered.** Be sure the phone number on the resume will, without exception, be answered by a person or an answering machine Monday through Friday 8 AM–5 PM.

EMPLOYMENT HISTORY GAPS

"What's wrong with a few gaps in my work history?" you might ask. "Isn't everyone entitled to a little time off?" Many responsible professionals have taken breaks in their careers to travel, take care of ill parents, recover from illness, and a myriad of other legitimate projects. But for some reason, employers don't like to see gaps in your work history.

If you have a period of unemployment in your history, here are some ways of dealing with it:

1. Use only years, not months, when referring to spans of time in your work history. This makes it quicker for the reader to grasp the length of time, and can eliminate the need to explain some gaps that occurred within two calendar years.

2. If your unemployment covers two calendar years or more, you need to explain the void. Consider all the things you were doing (volunteer work, school activities, internships, schooling, and travel) during that time and present them in terms that are relevant to your job objective if possible.

3. If your gap has no apparent relevance to your job objective, explain the gap honestly and with dignity. References to illness, unemployment (even if it is clearly due to a recession), and rehabilitation raise red flags in most cases, so avoid those at all cost. Speak about something else that you were doing during that time, even if it doesn't relate to your job objective. Suggested "job titles":
   - Full-time Parent
   - Home Management
   - Family Management
   - Family Financial Management
   - Independent Study
   - Personal Travel

WHAT NOT TO PUT ON A RESUME

- The word "Resume" at the top of the resume
- Fluffy rambling "objective" statements
- Salary information
- Full addresses of former employers
- Reasons for leaving jobs
- A "Personal" section, or personal statistics (except in special cases)
- Names of supervisors
- References

ACCURACY/HONESTY/STRETCHING THE TRUTH

Make sure that you can back up what you say. Keep the claims you make within the range of your own integrity. There is nothing wrong with pumping things up in your resume so that you communicate who you are and what you can do at your very best.

SOME ADDITIONAL ADVICE

1. Your resume is about your future; not your past.

2. It is not a confessional. In other words, you don't have to "tell all." Stick to what's relevant and marketable.

3. Don't write a list of job descriptions. Write achievements!

4. Promote only skills you enjoy using. Never write about things you don't want to repeat.

5. Be honest. You can be creative, but don't lie.

Your name
Mailing address
City, state, and zip
Telephone number(s)
Email address

Today's date

Your addressee's name
Professional title
Organization name
Mailing address
City, state and zip

Dear Mr. (or Ms.) last name,

Start your letter with a grabber—a statement that establishes a connection with your reader, a probing question, or a quotable quote. Briefly say what job you are applying for.

The mid-section of your letter should be one or two short paragraphs that make relevant points about your qualifications. You should not summarize your resume! You may incorporate a column or bullet point format here.

Your last paragraph should initiate action by explaining what you will do next (e.g., call the employer) or instigate the reader to contact you to set up an interview. Close by saying "thank you."

Sincerely yours,

Your handwritten signature

Your name (typed)

Enclosure: resume

Your Name
Address
Telephone #

Date

Dear _____,

I am pleased to submit this resume as application for the _____ position available with your company.

Since graduating from the _____ course at (the college name), I have continued to expand my skills and am currently preparing for the _____ certification exam.

I strive to perform to the best of my ability and my work ethic is based on being a conscientious, honest, and reliable employee. I believe that the training I have received as well as my compassion for the patient will enable me to become a productive team member with your company.

I truly enjoy helping people. This is one of the greatest assets I can bring to your company. This passion is reflected in my performance and contributes greatly to my success as well as the quality of care received by my patients.

Thank you for your time and consideration.

Respectfully,

[Your Name]
[Street Address], [City, ST ZIP Code]
[phone]
[e-mail]

Objective	*Medical Assistant/Technologist position for a private practice.*

Professional Experience	**Patient Service Technician/Unit Clerk** OAK TREE COMMUNITY HOSPITAL, Coronary Care Unit, Columbus, Indiana • Order lab work and x-rays • Prioritize patient daily care according to acuity and scheduled patient procedures • Assist patients with A.M. care, take vital signs, prep for procedures, draw blood, and obtain specimens • Maintain and set up patient rooms • Perform preventive maintenance on emergency equipment • Assist with patient and family education • Assist R.N. with sterile and non-sterile dressing changes • Perform EKGs • Trained in Phlebotomy • Utilize PC to enter and retrieve patient data • Answer multi-line phone, operate fax and copy machine **Office Assistant,** (6-month part-time position) GARTH FORT, M.D., Columbus, Indiana • Answered phone, scheduled patients • Greeted patients • Updated patient charts

---

Education	In-house training programs, *Oak Tree Community Hospital* EKG, 1993 Phlebotomy, 1993 Tech Class, 1992 Unit Clerk Class, 1990 Nursing Assistant Class, 1989 CPR Certified, since 1989 *Elm Tree Community College* Computer training: WordPerfect I, Certificate 1995 *Maple Grove State University* Major: Pre-Veterinarian, 1989–1990

POWER WORDS

Accomplish	Delegate	Innovate	Publish
Achieve	Demonstrate	Inspect	Qualify
Act	Design	Install	Raise
Adapt	Detail	Institute	Recommend
Administer	Determine	Instruct	Reconcile
Advertise	Develop	Integrate	Record
Advise	Devise	Interpret	Recruit
Aid	Direct	Interview	Rectify
Analyze	Distribute	Introduce	Redesign
Apply	Draft	Invent	Reduce
Approach	Edit	Investigate	Regulate
Approve	Employ	Lead	Relate
Arrange	Encourage	Maintain	Renew
Assemble	Enlarge	Manage	Report
Assess	Enlist	Manipulate	Represent
Assign	Establish	Market	Reorganize
Assist	Estimate	Mediate	Research
Attain	Evaluate	Moderate	Resolve
Budget	Examine	Modify	Review
Build	Exchange	Monitor	Revise
Calculate	Execute	Motivate	Scan
Catalogue	Exhibit	Negotiate	Schedule
Chair	Expand	Obtain	Screen
Clarify	Expedite	Operate	Select
Collaborate	Facilitate	Order	Sell
Communicate	Familiarize	Organize	Serve
Compare	Forecast	Originate	Settle
Compile	Formulate	Oversee	Solve
Complete	Generate	Perceive	Speak
Conceive	Govern	Perform	Staff
Conciliate	Guide	Persuade	Standardize
Conduct	Handle	Plan	Stimulate
Consult	Head	Prepare	Stimulate
Contract	Hire	Present	Summarize
Control	Identify	Preside	Supervise
Cooperate	Implement	Process	Support
Coordinate	Improve	Produce	Survey
Correct	Increase	Program	Synthesize
Counsel	Index	Promote	Systematize
Create	Influence	Propose	Teach
Decide	Inform	Provide	Train

The Phlebotomy Technician Program

THE INTERVIEW

YOU HAVE 5 MINUTES

That's why first impressions—being on time, being dressed appropriately and being prepared—are critical. If you make a bad first impression, it's going to be a lot harder for you to convince someone to hire you. The interview is the most important aspect of any job hunt. The impression you make on an employer will likely be the reason you get a job offer or not.

As mentioned previously, preparation is the key to any interview. The following guidelines will assist you in presenting a positive first impression:

1. **Look Sharp.**

   Before the interview, select your outfit. Depending on the industry and position, get out your best duds and check them over for spots and wrinkles.

2. **Be on Time.**

   Never arrive late to an interview. Allow extra time to arrive early in the vicinity, allowing for factors like getting lost. Enter the building 10 to 15 minutes before the interview.

3. **Do Your Research.**

   Research the company before the interview. The more you know about the company and what it stands for, the better chance you have of selling yourself.

4. **Be Prepared.**

Bring along a folder containing extra copies of your resume, a copy of your references and paper to take notes. You should also have questions prepared to ask at the end of the interview.

5. **Show Enthusiasm.**

A firm handshake and plenty of eye contact demonstrate confidence.

6. **Listen.**

One of the most neglected interviewing skills is *listening*.

7. **Answer the Question Asked.**

Candidates often don't think about whether or not they actually are answering the questions asked by their interviewers. Make sure you understand what is being asked, and get further clarification if you are unsure.

8. **Give Specific Examples.**

One specific example of your background is worth 50 vague stories. Prepare your stories before the interview. Give examples that highlight your successes and uniqueness.

9. **Ask Questions.**

Many interviewees don't ask questions and miss the opportunity to find out valuable information. Your questions indicate your interest in the company or job.

10. **Follow Up.**

Whether it's through email or regular mail, *the follow-up* is one more chance to remind the interviewer of all the valuable traits you bring to the job and company. You don't want to miss this last chance to market yourself.

INTERVIEWING SKILLS

Sell It to Me, Don't Tell It to Me

Interviews are the time to sell what you have accomplished, not simply to tell what you've done. Be prepared to give examples of your accomplishments to back up you statements. An example of this is: "In my current position I suggested a change in the scheduling which allowed greater utilization of our employees and reduced turn-around-time for our customers by 20%."

This is why it is vital that you practice your responses.

- Think of what questions the interviewer may ask and practice your answers. This will allow you to make sure that your answers are clear and concise and not long winded.
- Practice will also help to reduce some of your anxiety and increase your confidence level.
- Before the interview, think of your five best strengths. What makes them strengths? Think of examples in your past performance that provides proof of these strengths and what is the best way to convey this information to the person interviewing you.
- Every interview concludes with the interviewer asking if you have any questions. The worst thing to say is that you have no questions. Again be prepared. During your research of the company did any questions arise? Did any of the statements made by the person interviewing you, provide any questions? For example; during your research you learned that the company would be

expanding their outpatient facilities. This would provide an excellent opportunity to show your knowledge and interest in the future growth of the company by inquiring about this expansion.
- Never ask about benefits or salary during the interview process. The time for these questions is when the position has been offered to you.

COMMON INTERVIEW QUESTIONS

1. What are your strengths, assets, and things you do well and like about yourself?

2. What are your shortcomings, weaker points and areas for improvement?

3. Why should I hire you? How can you be an asset to this company?

4. Tell me about yourself.

5. Technical questions related to specific job functions.

6. What is your ideal coworker, supervisor or job environment?

HANDLING ILLEGAL QUESTIONS

Various federal, state, and local laws regulate the questions a prospective employer can ask you, the job candidate. An employer's questions—whether on the job application, in the interview, or during the testing process—must be related to the job you're seeking. For the employer, the focus must be: "What do I need to know to decide whether this person can perform the functions of this job?"

If asked an illegal question, you have three options:

- You can answer the question.
- You can refuse to answer the question, which is well within your rights.
- You can examine the question for its intent and respond with an answer as it might apply to the job. Let's say the interviewer asks, "Who is going to take care of your children when you are at work?" You might answer, "I can meet the work schedule that this job requires."

KEEPING TRACK OF IT ALL!

If you are keeping your promise and meeting the goal you set, you will accumulate quite a bit of data. It is important that all of this information be documented to ensure that you follow up on cold calls, cold visits, interviews etc. in a timely manner. The chart below will assist you in organizing your job search and keeping tract of those important contacts.

Job applied for	Company/contact Name	Phone/fax #	Date resume submitted	Follow up dates/comments

The Phlebotomy Technician Program

INTERVIEW FOLLOW UP

BE PERSISTENT—NOT A PEST

A thank you note or letter is a must when looking for a job. It will set you apart from the crowd as well as provide another opportunity to be front and center in the interviewer's mind.

Your thank you letter should use the same format and presentation as your resume. It should reiterate your skills and your interest in the position being offered.

THE RETURN CALL

If you don't get a return call as promised, call them and leave a message. Be prepared, professional and courteous. Try to reach the person at least once, explaining you want the information before you consider other positions because this company is your first choice. If you don't get an answer, consider it a "No." There is a fine line between being persistent and being a pest.

You may get lucky and actually reach the person when you call. If you do have such luck, use this opportunity to ask for feedback on your interview. Sometimes, not often, a person will take the time to give you advice. If this happens, be grateful and learn from the experience.

Name of person
The person's title
Name of company
Address

Date

Dear _____:

It was a pleasure to meet with you to discuss the position of _____.

I am very excited about the chance of becoming a productive member of your team. I am confident that the extensive _____ training I have already received will enable me to represent your company with integrity and skill.

During our discussion, I sensed your strong belief in providing quality service. I want to assure you of my conviction to this important task and I will strive to perform to this standard on a daily basis.

Thank you for this opportunity and I look forward to discussing the next step in the employment process soon.

Respectfully,

The Phlebotomy Technician Program

THE JOB SEARCH

WHERE DO I START?

Looking for employment is a full time job! Tough times call for tough strategies. Take the time to sit down and create a strategy including a commitment to call, mail a resume, or visit two places of employment a minimum of three days each week. Searching for a job can be discouraging and it's important that you set goals and stick with them!

- Go through the telephone book and make a list of every facility in your area that employs your qualifications
- Network with your family and friends and let everyone know you are looking for a job
- Call your references and let them know that you will be giving out their name again. No references lined up? Get some!
- Create or update your resume

COLD CALLS

If you find that your networking prospects are drying up, it may be time to think of new ways to penetrate the job market. The cold call is a basic technique used in selling, and when done properly, it can provide new opportunities for you. If the very thought of calling a stranger and selling yourself makes you cringe, you are not alone.

- Preparing a script to read from before making the call.
- Begin with a greeting—sounding enthusiastic (but not phony) will be a plus. Introduce yourself and say what your specialty is and how many years of experience you have in your field or any training you have received.
- Ask the magic question, 'When can I come in for an interview?"

Not everyone you call will be interested in what you're selling. Expect rejection; two out of every three calls will not lead to new prospects. But success is the result of trying. Your career will benefit from determination and consistent effort.

When looking for employment, persistence is the key. It is hard work but once you find that dream job it will be all worth the blood, sweat and yes those tears!

HOW FLEXIBLE ARE YOU?

Today's companies are seeking employees that possess not only the knowledge to perform multiple duties but also the willingness to multitask. The rising cost of healthcare requires that job functions be diverse and multifunctional. Candidates that show an interest in learning a new skill, performing several job functions, or working various shifts are much more attractive to the potential employer than someone not willing to bend in difficult times. Often positions are offered internally to current employees. Today's candidates need to be flexible. This may require a person to take a position that is less desirable in order to be eligible to apply for the preferred position once they are an employee.

According to the Bureau of Labor Statistics . . .

"Health care will generate 3 million new wage and salary jobs between 2008 and 2016, more than any other industry."

As the largest industry in 2006, health care provided 14 million jobs—13.6 million jobs for wage and salary workers and about 438,000 jobs for the self-employed. Also, 7 of the 20 fastest growing occupations are health care related. Most workers have jobs that require less than 4 years of college education, but health diagnosing and treating practitioners are among the most educated workers.

"ONCE I HAVE THE SKILLS, WHERE CAN I USE THEM?"

Public Hospitals	Primary Care Office
Medical Clinic	Private Hospitals
Rehab Hospital	Clinical laboratory
Independent Laboratory	Cardiology Practice
Hospital Pharmacy	Out Patient Rehab
Urgent Care Clinic	Multi-physician's Office
Home Health Care	Out Patient Laboratory
Hospice	Insurance Companies
Independent Pharmacy	Research Facility
Long-term-care Facilities	HMO's
Pharmaceutical Supply Company	Ambulatory Care Centers
Out Patient Surgery Center	Billing Company
Occupational Health	Radiology Facilities

Specialist's Office
Psychiatric Facility
VA Hospital
Pediatric Centers
Public Health Department
Chronic Care Facility
Physical Therapy Clinic
Medical Record Department

Ophthalmologist's Office
Acute Care Hospital
Cancer Centers
Birthing Center
Red Cross
Blood Banks
Sports Medicine Facility
Skilled Nursing Facility